FERRUCCIO CANA

Assisi

New practical guide

···ᐳ **6 itineraries to visit the town**

···ᐳ **200 color photos**

···ᐳ **Practical information**

···ᐳ **Plan of the town**

BONECHI EDIZIONI "IL TURISMO"

THE COMPLEX OF THE PILGRIMAGE CHURCH OF SAN FRANCESCO

History of the construction of the Franciscan complex

Little is known of the initial phases of the pilgrimage church of San Francesco in Assisi.

The place where the sanctuary church stands was still an isolated mound in the early 13th century, separated from the city by a drop in the land, where capital executions took place and where those condemned to death were publicly exposed. It was known as the *Colle dell'Inferno* or Hill of Hell. The construction of a large pilgrimage church became necessary when Francis was proclaimed saint in 1228, with all that this meant in the way of visits and pilgrimages to his sacred remains. In March the Pope donated part of the land on the Hill to Brother Elias for the building of the complex. In July the Pope himself laid the cornerstone, officially identifying the building as *ecclesia specialis*, a special church under the direct control of the Pope (a status it still retains).

What appears to the observer today as a highly articulated complex, capable of vying from a distance with the entire city of Assisi as it rises up in the landscape, is the fruit of enlargements over almost two centuries. What the original plans were is unknown.

On the basis of these few historical facts, the lower church has been dated to between 1228 and 1230, while the upper church may have been built under the General-

ship of Brother Elias (1232-1239), or later, between 1250 and 1260.

By the last decades of the 14th century most of the structures of the convent were in their definitive form. The 15th century, too, was a moment of great transformation for the convent wing of the church. Practically all the new and imposing structures of the south zone were built in the course of the century, notably enlarging the extension of the complex.

Subsequently to the fifteenth century, various parts of the Francis-

can complex were destroyed in the earthquakes which never let the city be for very long. The complex as we see it now is therefore the sum of the subsequent restorations and transformations. In the 18th century the two flights of steps from the lower Piazza to the area in front of the upper church were completed (the staircase actually dates back to the second half of the 16th century but not in its present form). Some of the small houses which stood right on the lower Piazza were torn down and the massive restorations of 1926 in this area completely modified the backdrop for those coming from the city gates. Three large windows on the side wall of the former Oratory of San Bernardino (it had already been transformed into a dormitory in the 17th century) were opened and the enclosure wall of the complex was torn down. Works carried out after the earthquake of 1997 on the other hand have tended to avoid redesigning the complex in any of its parts or to modify its appearance. Where possible, the precedent image has been restored while the static safety of the various structures has been ensured.

▼ Upper Church, facade

◄▲ Views of the complex of the Pilgrimage Church of San Francesco and the Lower Square

▲ The entrance to the Lower Church

▼ Narthex, the area going into the nave

THE LOWER CHURCH

The porch and the entrance. Entrance to the lower church is through a porch built by Francesco da Pietrasanta in the latter decades of the 15th century. The inscription in the frieze reads *"frater Franciscus Sanson generalis minorum fieri facit. 1487"*. The entrance portal has a central rose window with, below, two trilobate arches with a trumeau of small clustered columns between them. In the spandrel below the rose window is a mosaic with the *Blessing Saint Francis*, by some attributed to the Saint Francis Master, the late 13th

century artist who did so many of the frescoes in the lower church.

The narthex. After passing the great portal one enters the large narthex (or atrium or entrance bay), over 40 m long, which precedes the actual basilica.

The so-called *Chapel of San Sebastiano* opens off the left wall. This small space was created prior to 1542 and was then frescoed and decorated in 1646 with a canvas of the *Madonna and Child with Saint Sebastian* by Girolamo Martelli. Near the chapel, in the narthex, is a fresco of the *Madonna Enthroned with Saints (Anthony, Francis* on the left and *Rufinus* on the right) painted in 1422 by Ottaviano Nelli.

The fine monument on the right wall is known as the *Sepulcher of the Cerchi.*

Further on, along the right wall of the narthex, is a niche used as *cantoria*, commissioned in 1458 by the Nepis family of Assisi.

Next comes the *Monument to John of Brienne* (some say it is to Walter VI). Since the attribution of this monument depends primarily on the armorial bearings with the cross of Jerusalem to be seen on the base, some art historians suggest that it was a monument to *Philip di Courtenay*, who was also emperor of Constan-

tinople, and see the work as Gothic in style (perhaps by a pupil of Giovanni Pisano).

Chapel of Sant'Antonio abate. The chapel of Saint Anthony Abbot, founded shortly before 1360, contains late 14th century Gothic tombs. The frescoes by Pace di Bartolo that originally decorated the walls have been lost. One can go outside into the adjacent Chiostro dei Morti from this chapel.

Chiostro dei Morti or **Cemetery.** In 1492-93, during the Generalship of Francesco

▼ Narthex, the monument to John of Brienne

7

Nani known as Sansone, it was decided to renovate the old cemetery of the Franciscan complex.

Chapel of Santa Caterina. Back in the narthex of the lower church, on the right is the *Chapel of Saint Catherine*, which forms the head of the narthex. The chapel was commissioned by the Franciscan Third Order in 1343. In 1362 the papal legate of Castilian origin, Gil de Albornoz (1305-1367), commissioned Matteo Gattapone, an architect from Gubbio, in close contact with the Spanish ecclesiastic circles, to turn this space into his burial chapel. The stone facing on the walls and possibly the ribbed vaulting are apparently by Gattapone. In 1368 (a year after the legate's death), the Albornoz heirs commissioned the Bolognese painter Andrea de' Bartoli to fresco the chapel with the *Stories of Saint Catherine of Alexandria*, who was particularly venerated in the Middle Ages.

Figures of *Saints* and various scenes are frescoed on the intrados of the entrance arch to the chapel. On the right

▼ Narthex, Chapel of Santa Caterina

▲ Narthex, Chapel of Santa Caterina, Andrea de'Bartoli,
Saint Catherine before the Emperor Maxentius

they include the *Conversion of the Empress Faustina in Prison*, and the *Martyrdom of Faustina*. On the left are the *Martyrdom of Saint Catherine* and the *Death and Glory of the Saint*. Specific episodes in the *Life of Catherine* are shown in the wall panels, with, on the right from the bottom up, the *Conversion of Catherine* and *Catherine before the Emperor Maxentius*. On the left is the *Philosophical Dispute of Saint Catherine in Defense of the Faith* and then the *Martyrdom of the Christian Philosophers*.

9

THE NAVE

The frescoes on the walls of the lower church are perfect examples of a didactic itinerary planned for pilgrims visiting the tomb of the Saint. Between 1246 and 1266 the so-called Saint Francis Master, from Assisi, painted most of the frescoes on the walls of the great nave, one of the main cycles of 13th century Italian painting (the Master of the Blue Crucifixes also worked with him). The painter was commissioned to do a series of panels with episodes from the *Life of Saint Francis* which would stress the parallelism between the life of the Saint and that of Christ, a story in pictures that would accompany the devotional itinerary of the pilgrims.

► Lower Church, view of the nave

▲ Right wall, second bay,
Saint Francis Master, *Deposition* and, below,
Lamentation over the Body of Christ

RIGHT (or NORTH) WALL OF THE NAVE: the *Stories of Christ*

The opening of various chapels in the late 13th century unfortunately means that only a few fragments of the pictorial decoration of the *Life of Christ* have survived.

FIRST BAY

In the first bay the scenes, on the right, show the *Preparation of the Cross with Christ Stripped of His Garments* and, on the left, the *Crucifixion* (with *Christ Entrusting his Mother Mary to Saint John*).

SECOND BAY

On the right is the scene of the *Deposition* and on the left the *Lamentation over the Body of Christ.* In the *Lamentation* in particular, the Saint Francis Master achieves a high point in expressiveness in the careful rendering of textures. The body of *Christ* looks like polished ivory and sweeping folds of precious fabric envelop the figures of the pious women. To be noted also is the dynamically curving body of the grieving *Mary*.

THIRD BAY

The *Apparition of Christ* or the *Supper at Emmaus* (the second scene has been lost) is still visible. The damaged fresco below with the

▲ Third bay, view of the right wall

Madonna and Child dates to the latter part of the 1250s, and originally decorated the tomb of Cardinal Pietro di Barro.

LEFT (or SOUTH) WALL: the *Stories of Saint Francis*

FIRST BAY
The scenes in the first bay are, on the left, *Francis Renounces Worldly Possessions*, and on the right, the *Dream of Pope Innocent III*

▶ Left wall, first bay, Saint Francis Master, *Saint Francis Renounces Worldly Possessions*

◄ Left wall, second bay, Saint Francis Master, *Sermon to the Birds*

SECOND BAY

On the left is depicted the *Sermon to the Birds*, on the right, the *Stigmata of Saint Francis*

THIRD BAY

Shown is the scene with the *Funeral of the Saint and the Verification of the Stigmata.*

The tribune or pulpit of Saint Stanislas. A niche in the form of a cantoria (tribune or pulpit) dedicated to Saint Stanislas is now located in the wall. In 1337-1338

▲ Tribune or Cantoria of Saint Stanislas, Puccio Capanna

Puccio Capanna was called in to paint the space of this altar where mass was said in honor of Saint Stanislas, archbishop of Krakow, proclaimed saint in Assisi in 1253. At the back is the *Coronation of the Virgin with angelic choirs*, while in the soffit of the arch are two *Stories of Saint Stanislas: Stanislas Bringing a Dead Man Back to Life so He can Bear Witness to his Innocence before King Boleslas* and the *Martyrdom of the Saint*.

SANCTUARY (PRESBYTERY) AREA

VAULTS OF THE SANCTUARY: *the guiding principles to the teachings of Saint Francis*

▲ Tribune of Saint Stanislas, Puccio Capanna, *Martyrdom of the Saint*

Allegory of Poverty. In the center of the vault section, *Christ* takes the right hand of *Poverty* as she reaches it out to *Saint Francis* who, with divine benediction, is about to become her spouse. With her left hand, *Poverty* is offering a ring she has just received from *Hope*, while *Charity*, her head wreathed in roses, offers a heart to the newly wedded pair

Allegory of Purity or Chastity. In the vault towards the right transept, on the north, is the allegory of *Chastity*. She is shown enclosed in a castle, like the damsel of the chivalric poets, protected in the highest fortified tower, with two *Angels* bringing her a diadem and a palm, symbols of chastity.

The Glory of Saint Francis. *Saint Francis* is shown beardless as in early Christian depictions of Christ, his eyes wide open in mystical ecstasy. He is seated on a throne wearing splendid garments, surrounded by hosts of *Angels*, almost as if he were a new Messiah.

Allegory of Obedience. The allegory of Obedience shows her in a loggia placing a yoke on a kneeling *Friar*.

15

▲ Giottesque masters, *Allegory of Poverty* and *Allegory of Purity or Chastity*

16

▲ Giottesque masters, *Glory of Saint Francis* and *Allegory of Obedience*

ALTAR. The Gothic papal altar stands at the center of the sanctuary at the top of four steps. It was consecrated by Pope Innocent IV in 1253.

APSE. The apse vault as narrated by Giorgio Vasari and Brother Ludovico da Pietralunga, was frescoed until the 17th century with scenes of *Saint Francis in Glory and the Mission Entrusted by the Saint to the Minorites,* painted by Stefano Fiorentino, a pupil of Giotto. Because the frescoes were so deteriorated and difficult to interpret, in 1623 Cesare Sermei, at the time the best known artist in Assisi, was called in to replace them with the *Last Judgment* there now.

▼ Apse area, wooden choir stalls and fresco with the *Last Judgment* by Cesare Sermei

CHOIR STALLS. The choir stalls behind the altar were finished in 1471 (to which the signature on the right end bears witness). Two orders of stalls and back rests are carved with leaves and fantastic figures.

SOUTH OR LEFT TRANSEPT: *Stories of the Passion of Christ*

Chapel of San Giovanni Battista. According to Vasari, the Chapel of Saint John the Baptist, and that of Saint Nicholas in the north transept, were designed structurally by Agnolo and Agostino from Siena, active around the turn of the thirteenth century.

The frescoes in the transept. The main frescoes, of uncertain paternity, which Carlo

Volpe attributes to Lorenzetti when he had not yet achieved full artistic maturity, are the six in the transept vaulting. The cycle begins with the upper part of the vault, at the center. In the scene of the *Entry of Christ into Jerusalem*, the quality is exceedingly high,

In the panel of the *Last Supper*, the scene takes place inside a room shown in perspective, with illumination which contrasts with the dark outer world (on the left, above, the moon and stars).

The *Washing of the Feet* has been acknowledged as one of the most intense scenes in the cycle and is definitely thought to be by Pietro Lorenzetti himself.

The painter is particularly inventive in the dynamic poses of the group of figures in the

▲ South transept, Pietro Lorenzetti, the so-called *Sunset Madonna*, detail with Saint Francis

▼ View of the sanctuary and south transept

▲ South transept, Pietro Lorenzetti, *Last Supper*

center and the position of *Christ* in the *Flagellation.*

In the panel of the *Way to Calvary* Lorenzetti has paid particular attention to the depiction of the urban setting.

The frescoes unanimously attributed to Pietro Lorenzetti are those of the *Crucifixion* and the events that follow Christ's death.

The scene of the *Crucifixion* is the largest of all and occupies the space of four panels of the vault. Art historians are unanimous in considering this the high point of Lorenzetti's oeuvre, in particular because of the freedom and the "narrative power" of the sixty-five figures shown at the foot of the Cross.

This is followed by the *Deposition from the Cross,* the *Entombment,* the *Resurrection.*

For many scholars Lorenzetti's inventiveness diminished in the panel with the *Descent of Christ to Hell (Harrowing of Hell),* despite the fact that the meeting of the hand of *Christ* and that of the old *Adam* is a highly charged emotional moment.

Lorenzetti painted the scene of the *Stigmata of Francis* on the entrance staircase to the convent, a salient event in the identification of *Francis* with *Christ* (here shown instead of the Seraph) and the underlying motive behind the entire evangelical cycle in the transept. Lorenzetti's reference to Giotto in the landscapes is evident.

▲ South transept, Pietro Lorenzetti, *Washing of the Feet*

▲ South transept, Pietro Lorenzetti, *Crucifixion*

NORTH or RIGHT TRANSEPT:
Stories of the Childhood of Christ

The *Maestà with the Child Jesus Blessing Saint Francis* is in the second register above the entrance to the Chapel of the Magdalene.

Below the *Maestà* are five *Blessed Franciscans in Adoration* (the one in the center is frontal, those at the side in profile) which must have been part of the decoration of a 14th century altar. They were attributed to Pietro Lorenzetti by F.M. Perkins in 1908.

To the left of the *Maestà* is the *Crucifixion*, attributed to Giotto or his highly gifted pupils under his direction. Above, beginning with the third register, are a series of panels with the *Stories of the*

Childhood of Christ painted by Giotto's collaborators under his direction. They form one of the masterpieces of Italian 14th century painting. The *Annunciation* on the inner facade was painted by one of Giotto's assistants. The figures of the *Angel* and of *Mary* have been set at a distance from the opening of the chapel of San Nicola.

The *Visitation of Mary and Elisabeth*, attributed to Giotto, is on the vaulting. The *Nativity* scene, attributed by many to Giotto himself, is at the center of the vault.

In the panel on the right wall, above the *Crucifixion*, in the third register, is the *Epiphany* or *Adoration of the Magi*.

▼ View of the north transept

The *Presentation of Jesus in the Temple*, attributed to Giotto, is shown in the panel of the third register on the left.

On the vault, at the left, is the *Massacre of the Innocents*.

The *Flight to Egypt* is in the next panel, on the left wall.

In the *Christ among the Doctors*, the Temple of Jerusalem is depicted as the nave of a Gothic basilica to bring the event into the present time. This is one of the most skillful forerunners of the one-point perspective which was developed in the 15th century.

In the third register on the left, interrupted by the entrance to the cloister outside, is *Jesus Leaving the City of Jerusalem and Returning to Nazareth*.

The scenes frescoed on the walls in the second register, along the line of the *Maestà* and the *Crucifixion*, depict some of the best known miracles of Saint Francis and children. There is the *Boy of Suessa Taken out of the Ruins of a House* (note the perspective rendering of the building and the arched movement of the weeping women) and the *Boy of Suessa Resuscitated by Saint Francis*.

On the left wall, near the stairs leading to the cloister above, on the right is a

▼ North transept, Cimabue,
Madonna and Child in Majesty

▲ North transept, Giotto, *Crucifixion*

scene with *Saint Francis and Death*, in which the figure of the saint is highly realistic. On the left is the *Miracle of a Child who was Unhurt after Falling from the Top of a House.*

Chapel of San Nicola. The Chapel of Saint Nicholas opens in the back wall, north of the transept. It was built by Cardinal Napoleone Orsini in memory of his brother Gian (Giovanni) Gaetano, who died during the conclave of 1292-1294. In the barrel vault, from top to bottom, *Saint Nicholas Giving the Maidens of Pantera a Dowry (throwing three golden balls* or rods); *Saint Nicholas Saving some Sailors from a Storm* (lost scene); *Saint Nicholas Receiving Three Roman Knights in Myra* or *Blessing a penitent with a rope around his neck who is kneeling before him.*

On the barrel vault, on the left, *Saint Nicholas Saving Three Innocents from Decapitation. Sailors Pouring the Oil Dedicated to Diana into the Sea, Saint Nicholas Appearing to Constantine in a Dream.* Next come two *Apostles.* On the side walls the miracles of the Saint continue with on the right *Saint Nicholas Bringing a Child Back to Life, Saint Nicholas*

25

Freeing the Slave Adeodatus, Saint Nicholas Returning Adeodatus to his Parents.

Only one scene remains on the left wall: *An Elderly Jew Striking the Image of the Saint.*

Above the entrance arch, on the inner facade, are *Saint Francis and Saint Nicholas Presenting Giovanni Gaetano and Napoleone Orsini to Christ,* shown blessing within a shrine.

On the back wall is the *tomb of Giovanni Gaetano Orsini,* who died in 1292 but was not brought here until 1296.

▼ North transept, Chapel of San Nicola

▲ North transept, Chapel of San Nicola, the Orsini Tomb

THE CHAPELS ON THE RIGHT SIDE

Chapel of Santa Maria Maddalena. The *Magdalene* cycle on the walls begins in the lower register of the wall to the left of the entrance, and continues on the right wall and then the lunette.

To be noted on the left: the portrait of *Teobaldo Pontano, Supper of Christ and Mary Magdalene in the House*

▼ Chapel of Santa Maria Maddalena, Giotto, *Supper in the House of the Pharisee*

of the Pharisee, the *Raising of Lazarus*, undoubtedly one of the finest scenes, assigned to Giotto, for the style is close to that of the Scrovegni Chapel in Padua. *Trans-* *portation of Mary Magdalene to Heaven*.

On the right wall: the "*Noli me tangere*".

The Journey of Saint Mary Magdalene to Marseilles.

Mary Magdalene Speaking with the Angels. Mary Magdalene Receiving the Vestments from the Hermit Zosimus.

▼ Chapel of Santa Maria Maddalena, Giotto, *the Saint with Teobaldo Pontano, the dedicatee*

THE CHAPELS ON THE LEFT SIDE

Chapel of San Martino. The fresco decoration on the walls, about which we have no certain information but which was assigned by Cavalcaselle to Simone Martini, was painted between 1317 and 1320. Vasari assigns the paintings in this Chapel to Puccio Capanna, but by the 18th century art historians tended to ascribe them to Simone Martini. For decades the date has also been a moot question: some say 1315-1317, some 1320, some 1324-1326, some 1328-1333, and some 1330-1335. At present critics prefer the earlier date of 1315-1317.

Eight *Saints*, full figure, are shown in the soffit of the entrance arch, among whom *Saint Clare* and *Saint Catherine* in particular can be noted. On the walls are the *Stories of Saint Martin*, a saint who can be compared to Francis in various episodes (in particular the episode in which *Francis is Honored by a Simple Man* and above all *Francis Giving his Cloak to a Poor Man*).

▼ View of the entrance to the Chapel of San Martino

As in the Chapel of Saint Mary Magdalene, the cycle begins in the lowest register, from left to right.

Saint Martin Dividing his Mantle with a Poor Man at the Gates of Amiens.

Christ Appears to Saint Martin in a Dream Holding the Cloak He had Given Away.

Emperor Julian Knights Martin.

Saint Martin Renounces Arms and Confronts the Enemy Armed with a Cross.

Saint Martin, Deep in Meditation, Is Shaken by a Cleric.

The Emperor Valentinian Paying Homage to Saint Martin: The Miracle of Fire.

On the vault are: *The Dream of Saint Ambrose Predicting the Death of Saint Martin* (or the *Meditation of Saint Martin*).

In the scene of the *Death of Saint Martin* the body of the saint is placed, in homage to his humble life style, on the bare ground (which ties in

▼ Chapel of San Martino, Simone Martini, *Death of Saint Martin*

with the particular devotion of Saint Francis to Poverty), despite the richness of his garment.

Saint Martin's Funeral Rites
This is one of the finest scenes in the cycle in the Chapel.

Back in the main nave, one can go down into the Crypt.

CRYPT. Even though the search for the mortal remains of the saint lasted centuries, it was not until 1818 that Pope Pius VII announced the finding of the body and crowds flocked to Assisi. It was then decided to dig the third church and use it as a crypt for the complex. The tomb of Jacopa dei Settesoli is in the entrance vestibule where the two flights of steps begin.

In the nave, at the center, is the altar beyond which, behind an iron grill, is the stone urn which contains the remains of Saint Francis. In the niches at the sides are the remains of the first four companions of Francis; Rufino, Angelo, Masseo and Leone.

Back up at the top turn towards the right transept and from there into the Chapter Hall.

CHAPTER HALL or Chapel of the Relics. In the northern transept, to the left of the Chapel of Saint Nicholas, is a

▲ Crypt, the tomb of Saint Francis

door which leads to the Chapter Hall, in the oldest wing of the monastic complex, the papal part dating to 1230-1240. The room is square in plan with groin vaulting which springs from the massive pylon at the center. One of the most interesting 14th century frescoes in Assisi is to be found here: the *Crucifixion and the Saints* executed by Puccio Capanna around 1340.

The hall is now used as a chapel for the most precious relics of Saint Francis.

The *Rule* is the manuscript of the final authorization for the life of the Franciscan Order imposed by Pope Honorius III in 1223.

◄ Convento di San Francesco,
Chapter Hall,
Puccio Capanna,
Crucifixion

The *tunic* is the one Francis wore: the coarse sheep's wool cloth bears witness to his ideal of extreme Poverty. The *Benediction imparted by Francis to Brother Leone* is a document dictated by Francis in 1224, in answer to some of Leo's questions. Leo was one of the followers

▼ Convento di San Francesco, Chapter Hall, the *Franciscan Rule of 1223*

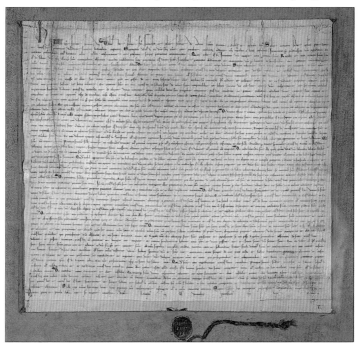

▶ Convento of San Francesco, Chapter Hall, the *Benediction imparted by Francesco to Brother Leone*

who, unlike the other brothers, was not sure of how he was to behave with regards to the evangelical precept of extreme poverty.

Back in the transept the staircases lead to the Chiostro Grande

CHIOSTRO GRANDE. The columns of the cloister are decorated with capitals which mirror late 15th century ornamental fashions while inside, on the lunettes, are frescoes in green earth painted between 1564 and 1570 by Dono Doni with episodes from the *Stories of Saint Francis*. Their state of conservation is highly precarious.

▼ View of the Chiostro Grande

MUSEO DEL TESORO. Entrance to the Museo del Tesoro or Treasury Museum is from the Chiostro Grande. The museum is located on the upper floor of the cloister in the "Sala Gotica", and houses some of the works donated in the course of centuries to the basilica, including various unique examples of French 13th century goldwork.

◄ Convento di San Francesco, Museo del Tesoro, Master of the Blue Crucifixes, *Crucifix*

▲ Convento di San Francesco, Museo del Tesoro, Maestro del Tesoro, *Saint Francis and four of his miracles*

PERKINS COLLECTION. This important collection of Italian art, dating from the 14th to the 16th century, was given to the Sacro Convento by the American art historian Fredrick Mason Perkins (1874-1955), who spent years studying the frescoes in the upper and lower churches. These 57 works, mostly on panel, are a representative selection of the various regional schools (Umbrian, Sienese, Florentine, Venetian, Emilian). Of particular note are works by Pietro Lorenzetti, Fra Angelico, Signorelli.

▶ Convento di San Francesco, Perkins Collection, Masolino da Panicale, *Madonna and Child* (15th cent.)

UPPER CHURCH

TRANSEPT. The transept of the upper church consists of the sanctuary or presbytery bay and two side bays (north and south) forming the arms of the transept.

SOUTH ARM. The frescoes on the south arm of the transept were painted after those in the north transept (1265-1268), together with the vault sections of the sanctuary (1278-1280), by Cimabue and his assistants.

▼ View of the south transept

SOUTH-EASTERN WALL. The wall is divided into three registers, as are those in the nave, and the narration begins in the lowest register with the *Crucifixion*, one of the most intensely dramatic scenes of Cimabue's art.

Next come the *Angels* (middle register) and then, above, the *Glory of Christ in Heaven* to conclude his earthly life.

SOUTH WALL. Because of the large four-light window, the wall is divided into only two registers, with the *Angels* on either side of the opening in the upper register. Below, the wall of the bay is subdivided into three

▲ South transept, the four-light window

▼ South transept, south-east wall, Cimabue, *Crucifixion*

panels, just as in the nave with the *Franciscan Stories*, stressing the compositional as well as theological unity. In the left scene is the *Vision of the Throne and the Book of Seven Seals*.

At the center is the *Vision of the Angels at the Four Corners of the Earth*.

On the right, the *Apocalyptic Christ, Judge of Men* surrounded by seven *Angels* with their trumpets calling the *elect* (among which are many Franciscans).

SOUTH-WEST WALL. In the three registers on the wall are: above, in the lunette, the apocalyptic episode of the *Three Archangels Defeating the Dragon* (that is Evil); in the middle gallery (walkway) register, *Angels*; in the lower register, respectively, on the left the *Fall of Babylon*, while on the right is the *Vision of Heavenly Jerusalem of Saint John in Patmos*.

Cimabue touches one of the summits of his art in the *Fall of Babylon*.

▼ South transept, south wall, Cimabue, *Apocalyptic Christ*

SANCTUARY

APSE. The apse is divided into three registers, and the middle register separates the *Stories of the Childhood of Mary* from those following the *Death of Christ*.

The three two-light windows in the apse are particularly important because they are among the few examples of medieval Italian stained glass that have come down to us.

Inside an aedicule at the center of the apse is the *papal throne*, made by Roman marble workers around the middle of the 13th century.

ALTAR. The *high altar* was consecrated in 1253 by Pope Innocent IV.

▼ View of the apse zone

◄ Nave and sanctuary, the vault rebuilt "neutrally" after the earthquake of 1997

▼ Sanctuary, Cimabue, vault with the *Evangelists* before the earthquake

CROSSING VAULTS: the *Evangelists*

The four vault sections above the sanctuary act as a connecting link between the *Stories of the Life of the Virgin* in the apse and the *Via Sacra* in the nave in expressing the history of the Church. The vaults are frescoed with figures of the *Four Evangelists*, who wrote the four books of the *Gospels*, the only neo-testamentary Sacred Scriptures recognized by the Church as the story of the teachings of Christ.

► North transept,
the four-light window

The vaults were painted, according to the art historians, by the Florentine painter Cimabue. On the north side we have the section with the figure of *Saint Mark* and of "*Ytalia*", with reference specifically to Rome and its monuments.

In the west section, adjacent to the apse, is *Saint Luke* with reference to Greece (indicated as "*Ipn-acchaia*" as was customary in the Middle Ages) and, in particular, Corinth.

On the south side is the section with the figure of *Saint John*, who spread Christianity in Asia (the reference here is to the city of *Ephesos*, now in Turkey).

The east vault adjacent to

▼ Apse, the papal throne and the choir stalls before the earthquake of 1997

▲ View of the north transept

▲ North transept, north-west wall, Cimabue, *Saint Peter Healing the Lame Man*

the nave with the figure of *Saint Matthew* and *Judea* (with Jerusalem) is unfortunately the one that fell in the earthquake of 1997.

CHOIR STALLS. The wooden choir stalls, which run along the entire western wall of the basilica, are a fine example of late 15th century cabinet work.

NORTH ARM. Apparently it was Pope Clement IV (1265-1268), closely tied to the house of Anjou, who first commissioned the frescoes in the north arm of the transept.
The work of a talented painter in the French style, with assistants, has been identified in the upper zones.

NORTH-WEST WALL. The wall once more is divided into three registers. In the uppermost one is *God in Majesty Surrounded by the Symbols of the Evangelists*.

After the figures of the *Angels* on high and the *Apostles* further down, in the middle register, to mediate between Heaven and earth, are scenes of the *Life of Saint Peter*, designated by Christ as founder of the Church ("you are Peter and on this stone I will found my Church"). Left, *Peter Healing a Lame Man* by Cimabue. On the right, *Peter Heals the Sick and Liberates Those Possessed from Demons* by Cimabue. *Peter*, at the center of the scene, raises his arm and miracles are accomplished by this gesture.

▼ North transept, north wall, Cimabue, *Martyrdom of Saint Peter*

NORTH WALL. In the highest register on the north wall, on either side of the large quadrifore, are the *prophet Elijah* on the left and *King David* on the right.

The S*tories of Saint Peter* continue in the register below with the addition of the stories of *Saint Paul*, the "Apostle of the people". Francis was particularly devoted to both of them.

On the left, the *Fall of Simon Magus*, where the kneeling *Saint Paul* is shown as well as *Saint Peter*. At the center is the *Martyrdom of Saint Peter*.

On the right the *Martyrdom of Saint Paul* (fragmentary) is shown.

NORTH-EAST WALL. The lowermost register is taken up by the *Crucifixion* with *Longinus*, who was then converted and became a Saint, as a symbol of the redemption of the pagans. On the right is *Saint Francis* embracing the Cross. In this scene Cimabue has given us the moment of the verification of the death of *Christ*, as compared to the corresponding scene in the south transept where *Christ* is still alive and entrusts *Mary* to *John*, with *Longinus* who touches Christ's ribs with his lance (inflicting a stigma).

▼ North transept, north-east wall, Cimabue, *Crucifixion*

THE NAVE: *Saint Francis and the concordance between the Old and New Testaments*

RIGHT (or NORTH) WALL OF THE NAVE: *the continuity between the History of the People of Israel and the Franciscan Message*

FOURTH BAY - Horizontal reading: *the life of Saint Francis*

◄ scene I, Giotto, *Saint Francis Honored by a Simple Man*

◄ scene II, Giotto, *Saint Francis Gives His Cloak to a Poor Man*

► scene III, Giotto,
*The Dream
of the Palace
Filled with Arms
in Spoleto*

◄ Nave, fourth bay,
view of the north wall

Vertical reading:
*the Old Testament
and Saint Francis*

First register above divided by the window: on the left the *Creation of the World* (or the *Separation of light from dark* by Jacopo Torriti) and, on the right, the *Creation of Adam* by Jacopo Torriti.

Middle register divided by the window: left: *Noah Building the Ark* (by Jacopo Torriti) and, right, *Noah going into the Ark* (or *The Flood* by Jacopo Torriti).

47

THIRD BAY - Horizontal reading: *the life of Saint Francis*

◀ scene IV, Giotto,
*Saint Francis
Praying
in the Church
of San Damiano*

◀ scene V, Giotto,
*The Renouncement
of Worldly Goods*

► scene VI, Giotto, *The Dream of Pope Innocent III*, in which he recognizes the mission of Francis who is supporting the Lateran Basilica

◄ Nave, third bay, view of the north wall

Vertical reading: *the Old Testament and Saint Francis*

First register above divided by the window: on the left the *Creation of Eve* (Jacopo Torriti) and, on the right, the *Original Sin* (Jacopo Torriti).

Middle register divided by the window: on the left the *Sacrifice of Abraham* (Jacopo Torriti or the young Giotto) and, on the right, the *Angels visit Abraham* (the obvious repainting of this scene make any hypothesis as to the original artist impossible).

49

VAULT OVER THE THIRD BAY: *the origins of the primitive Church and of the new Church*

In the west vault, towards the sanctuary, is *Christ the Redeemer*. On the south is *Mary*. The image of *Saint Francis* appears in the east vault, in the direction of the main entrance. Towards the north is *Saint John the Baptist*.

► View of the nave towards the inner facade after the restorations subsequent to the 1997 earthquake

▲ Upper Church, view of the nave

SECOND BAY - Horizontal reading: *the life of Saint Francis*

◄ scene VII, Giotto,
*Pope Innocent III
orally approves
the Franciscan
rule and gives
his blessing*

◄ scene VIII, Giotto,
*The Apparition
of the Fiery Chariot
at Rivotorto,
like the early
prophet Elijah*

► scene IX, Giotto,
*Brother Pacifico
has the Vision
of the Heavenly
Thrones with One
for Francis*

◄ Second bay,
middle register, Isaac
Master (the young Giotto),
Isaac blessing Jacob

Vertical reading:
*the Old Testament
and Saint Francis*

First register above divided
by the window: on the left
Expulsion from Paradise
(Jacopo Torriti?) and, on the
right, the *Labors of Adam
and Eve* (destroyed).
Middle register divided by
the window: on the left *Isaac
blessing Jacob* (or *Jacob's
deception* by the Isaac Master or the young Giotto) and,
on the right *Esau before
Isaac* (*Isaac driving away
Esau*, by the Isaac Master or
the young Giotto).

53

FIRST BAY - Horizontal reading: *the public life of Saint Francis*

◄ scene X, Giotto,
*Francis establishes
peace in the city
driving the demons
from Arezzo,
that is defeating
the Ghibellines*

◄ scene XI, Giotto,
*Francis survives
the ordeal by fire
before the sultan
of Egypt, a sign
of the superiority
of Christianity*

► scene XII, Giotto,
*The ecstasy
of Francis and the
acknowledgment
of Christ's support
of his mission*

◄ Nave, first bay,
view of the north wall

Vertical reading:
*the Old Testament
and Saint Francis*

First register above divided by the window: on the left the *Sacrifice of Cain and Abel* (destroyed) and, on the right, the *Killing of Abel* (fragmentary).

Middle register divided by the window: left *Joseph thrown into the well by his brothers* (or *Joseph sold*, by the Pentecost Master or the young Giotto) and, on the right, *Joseph reveals himself to his brothers* (or *Joseph's brothers in Egypt are pardoned by him*, by the Pentecost Master or the young Giotto).

VAULT OVER THE FIRST BAY: *the Fathers of the Church*

In the vault on the west, towards the sanctuary, is *Saint Gregory the Great*. On the north is *Saint Augustine*. The figure of *Saint Jerome*, which was in the east section of the vault near the main entrance, fell in the earthquake of 1997. On the south is *Saint Ambrose*; below the vault before the quake.

OPEN VESTIBULE: *the life of Saint Francis*

◀ scene XIII, on the right-hand corner, near the entrance. Giotto, *The Crib in Greccio* or *the Reenactment of the Manger Scene with the Coronation of the Christ Child*

LEFT WALL: *the identification of Francis with Christ and the problem of the stigmata*

OPEN VESTIBULE: *the life of Saint Francis*

◀ scene XVI, at the left-hand corner, near the entrance. Giotto, *The Death of the Knight of Celano*

INNER FACADE - Horizontal reading: *the life of Saint Francis*

◄ scene XIV, Giotto, *The Miracle of the Spring or Saint Francis bringing forth a new source of water*

◄ Scene XV, Giotto, *The Sermon to the Birds*

▶ Nave,
inner facade,
Giotto, *Ascension
of Christ*

◀ Nave, view of the
inner facade before
the earthquake of 1997

Vertical reading:
*the Church
and Saint Francis*

First register above be-
neath the rose window: on
the right is the *Ascension
of Christ*, when *Christ* rises
to Heaven, in the presence
of Mary and the Apostles.
On the left is *Pentecost*,
showing the descent of the
Holy Spirit in the form of
tongues of fire on the
Apostles.
Middle register above the
entrance doors: on the left
is Saint Peter, at the center the *Madonna and
Child*, and, on the right,
Saint Paul.

LEFT (or SOUTH) WALL OF THE NAVE

FIRST BAY - Horizontal reading: *the life of Saint Francis*

◄ scene XVII,
Giotto, *Francis
preaching before
Pope Honorius III
or The Last
Franciscan Rule*

◄ scene XVIII,
Giotto,
*The Apparition
of Francis to
the Brothers and
to Saint Anthony
preaching in the
Chapter in Arles*

► scene XIX, Giotto, *Francis receiving the stigmata on Monte La Verna*

◄ Nave, first bay, view of the south wall

Vertical reading: *Saint Francis and episodes of the Life of Christ*

First register above divided by the window: on the right the *Dispute in the Temple* (fragmentary); on the left, the *Baptism of Jesus in the Jordan* (fragmentary)
Middle register divided by the window: on the right, *Lamentation over the Dead Christ* (attributed to Giotto); left, the *Three Marys at the Sepulcher* (fragmentary).

61

SECOND BAY - Horizontal reading: *the death of Saint Francis*

◄ scene XX,
Giotto, the *Death
of Saint Francis
and the vision
of his ascension
to heaven*

◄ scene XXI,
Giotto,
*The Apparition
of Saint Francis to
Brother Agostino
and the Bishop
of Assisi*

► scene XXII,
Giotto,
*The confirmation
of the stigmata
on the body
of Francis
by a lay person*

◄ Nave, second bay,
view of the south wall

Vertical reading:
*the death
of Saint Francis
and the death of Christ*

First register above divided by the window: on the right the *Presentation in the Temple for the circumcision* (Maestro della Cattura); left, *Flight into Egypt* (fragmentary).
Middle register divided by the window: right, *Christ on his Way to Calvary* (Maestro della Cattura); left, *Crucifixion* (perhaps by a Tuscan painter).

63

THIRD BAY - Horizontal reading: *mourning the death of Francis and his canonization*

◄ scene XXIII, Giotto, *Mourning of the Poor Clares and the leave-taking of Clare from the body of Francis*

◄ scene XXIV, Giotto, *Canonization of Saint Francis*

▶ scene XXV,
Giotto,
*Saint Francis
appears to Pope
Gregory IX
who was initially
incredulous
of the reality
of the stigmata
and is now
convinced
by the Saint*

◀ Nave, third bay,
view of the south wall

Vertical reading:
*Saint Francis
and episodes
of the Life of Christ*

First register above divided by the window: on the right the *Nativity* (or the *Manger Scene* by the Maestro della Cattura); left, *Adoration of the Magi* (or *Epiphany*, fragmentary).
Middle register divided by the window: right, *Capture of Christ* (or the *Betrayal of Judas* by the Maestro della Cattura); left, *Christ before Pilate* (or the *Flagellation*, fragmentary).

65

FOURTH BAY - Horizontal reading: *the miracles of the Franciscan faith*

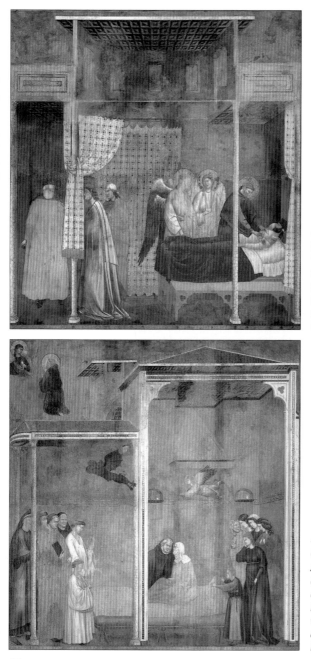

◄ scene XXVI,
Giotto,
*The miracles
of Saint Francis
in foreign lands:
the healing
of John of Lerida
in Catalonia*

◄ scene XXVII,
Giotto,
*A Franciscan friar
confesses a woman
on Monte Merano
in Benevento,
who was dead
and has just come
back to life*

► scene XXVIII, Giotto, *Saint Francis liberates Peter of Alife who had been unjustly accused of heresy and imprisoned*

◄ Nave, fourth bay, view of the south wall

Vertical reading: *the miracles of Saint Francis and those of the Life of Christ*

First register above divided by the window: on the right the *Annunciation* (perhaps by Jacopo Torriti); left, the *Visitation* (destroyed)

Middle register divided by the window: right, the *Wedding of Cana* (perhaps by Jacopo Torriti, but the obvious repainting makes any real hypothesis as to the artist impossible); left, the *Resurrection of Lazarus* (perhaps by Jacopo Torriti, fragmentary).

67

FROM THE BASILICA OF SAN FRANCESCO TO THE PIAZZA DEL COMUNE

**Porta San Francesco • Abbey of San Pietro • Fonte Marcella
Monastery of San Giuseppe • Basilica of Santa Maria Maggiore
Bishop's palace • Oratory of San Francescuccio
Oratory of San Francesco Piccolino • Chiesa Nuova**

Entry is from the Piazza Inferiore or lower piazza of the Basilica of San Francesco, through Via Frate Elia after the narrow passageway through the city gate.

In the 14th century this was already an area in which pilgrims traditionally found accommodation. In the 19th century, with the development of tourism, it became one of the principal poles for the urban expansion of Assisi. The accommodation potentialities for tourists were increased with the building in 1868 of the Hotel Subasio, the Hotel Giotto in 1900 and the Hotel Windsor Savoia in 1911.

Beyond the narrow passageway that closes the lower square of San Francesco and that has always been known as the "Old Postern Gate of San Francesco" and which led into the convent area, stands a shrine with the fresco of the *Immaculate Conception*.

▼ View of Assisi from the Upper Church

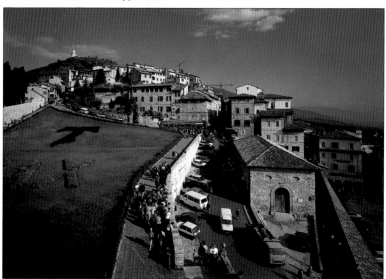

Porta San Francesco

The Porta San Francesco currently consists of a tower with neo-medieval 'Guelph' battlements To be noted in the archway are the coats of arms of the city and of Pope Urban IV, painted in 1367 by Pace di Bartolo. Prior to the 19th century, the walls, like the urban gates, were plastered, painted and frescoed, an integral part of the multi-colored aspect of the old cities.

▲ Porta San Francesco, coats of arms

Porta San Pietro

Porta San Pietro (St. Peter's Gate) is reached by crossing the Piazzale dell'Unità d'Italia. It too was crowned by Guelph crenellations on the tower at the turn of the nineteenth century.

Abbey of San Pietro

The facade of the abbey church of San Pietro stands at the end of Piazza San Pietro. Formerly at a considerable distance from the city walls, it found itself right next to the new walls after their enlargement in 1316.

First mention of the building dates to 1029 (although some scholars refer to a Benedictine foundation of 970).

In 1268 the building was modified again, as stated in the long inscription in the band under the corbel table.

A large portal surrounded by Romanesque plant motifs stands in the center of the lower tier, with two stone lions before it.

The top of the building has a straight corbel table, like the one below, although up to 1832 it had a steep triangular pediment (destroyed in an earthquake) which clearly related this building to others in Spoleto as well as to

▼ A typical street in the center of Assisi

the facade of the cathedral of San Rufino.

The interior, now very bare and without its original frescoes, is divided into a nave and two aisles separated by piers. The nave has a timber ceiling supported by ogival stone arches. In the 19th century this had already been identified as a typical feature of medieval Umbrian churches and was then extended to the early Franciscan buildings (Biebrach). To be noted over the aisles are the tunnel vaults which may also date to the fifteenth century.

The presbytery is raised because of the crypt below. It has a small cupola in false dome structure with each row of ashlars projecting more than the one below (this was also customary in Provence in the 13th century).

The *Chapel of the Madonna del Rosario* with a canvas dating to 1611, to the left of the main entrance, is all that remains of the 17th century.

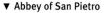
▼ Abbey of San Pietro

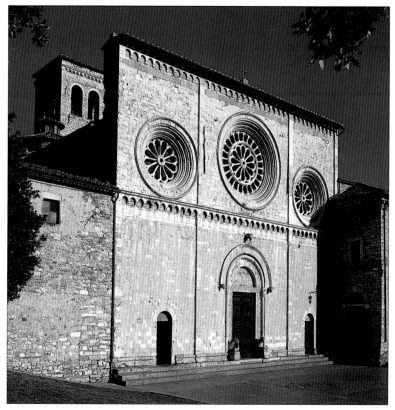

Near the sanctuary, where an early medieval sarcophagus with *San Vittorino martyr* (an old patron of Assisi) has been reused beneath the high altar, are two interesting rooms which would seem to indicate that the original layout of the basilica is of very early date, perhaps when Byzantine Assisi was desperately attempting to hold out against the Lombard king Totila (545-546).

There are also interesting 13th century frescoes, which have been related by some to the court of Frederick II, such as the *saints* and the band with hunting scenes. It is no coincidence that the original facade (prior to 1253) was inspired by buildings in Spoleto, "the" imperial city in Umbria and the temporary residence of the emperor.

Fonte Marcella
(Via Fontebella)

The Fonte Marcella is set against the so-called Monte Frumentario in the point in which the street widens out. It was commissioned in 1556 (on behalf of the pope) by the Sienese governor of Assisi Marcello Tutu after whom it is named.

The stairs opposite lead to Via del Pozzo and from there to Borgo San Pietro, which continues in Via Sant'Apollinare.

▲ Fonte Marcella

Monastery and Church of San Paolo and Sant'Apollinare or Monastery of San Giuseppe

In 1452 the two older convent complexes of San Paolo dating to 1341 and Sant'Apollinare dating to 1286, once separated by a lane, were joined to form the monastery of San Giuseppe. Inside, the *parlatorium* of the cloistered convent has interesting remains of 14th century paintings, to be seen in relation to the frescoes in the basilica of San Francesco. *Sant'Apollinare Enthroned* and *Saint Michael Archangel* have been attributed to one of the Masters of the Vaulting in the sanctuary of the lower church. In the former nun's choir are an *Annunciation* and a *Cruci-*

▲ Monastery of San Giuseppe,
Puccio Capanna, *Annunciation*

fixion which are considered some of Puccio Capanna's best works and date to a period following that of his training in the ranks of Giottesque painters, at work in the decoration of the vaults of the lower church. The picture of *Saint Francis Receiving the Stigmata* is linked to Pace di Bartolo, in the second half of the 14th century (he had done frescoes in the chapel of Sant'Antonio in the lower church of San Francesco).

Continuing towards Piazza Vescovado, on the left is the steep Via Giovanni Bonino.

Basilica of Santa Maria Maggiore and the presumed **House of the Latin poet Sextus Propertius**

The church of Santa Maria Maggiore, first bishop's seat in the city, seems to have been built in the 4th century on the site of a temple of Janus (to Christianize a site of pagan worship). In the 9th century the building was completely transformed by adding a crypt, while in 1035 it was decided to move the title of cathedral of Assisi to San Rufino.

In subsequent centuries the building continued to be enlarged and modified. In 1162 a new facade was built by an architect who seems to have come from Gubbio (it may have been the same Giovanni who also worked in the Cathedral), while traditionally Francis appears to have offered advice regarding the transformation of the apse zone (we know that Francis was particularly interested in the restoration of religious buildings).

The earthquake of 1832 seriously damaged Santa Maria Maggiore, and the right aisle and a good part of the facade collapsed. The facade there now was built in 1938. To be noted in the main portal is the fragment of the basin of a Roman fountain.

The interior, on a basilica plan, is divided into a nave and two aisles. As was customary in medieval Umbrian architecture, the nave is covered by a wooden ceiling, while the side aisles are covered in brick vaulting (that over the left aisle probably dates to the 12th century,

while that over the right aisle was redone, on the example of the other, during a rather unsuccessful restoration of 1940).

An early Christian sarcophagus decorated with the typical vine shoots and dating to the 8th century is set against the inner facade. Remains of the frescoes which decorated much of the walls up to the earthquake of 1832 can still be seen along the walls of the nave, the apse and the sacristy. Of particular note is a *Pietà* apparently by Tiberio d'Assisi (1470-1524) in the left aisle and a late 14th century *Madonna and Saints* by the so-called San Leonardo Master on the first pier to the left. Note also the mid 14th century decoration by Pace di Bartolo, including an *Annunciation* on the left wall.

The crypt, beneath the high altar, is divided by columns with fine reused Roman capitals. There was a passage, now closed, from the crypt to a large Roman house, probably belonging to someone of high lineage, perhaps even the poet Sextus Propertius.

▼ Basilica of Santa Maria Maggiore

Bishop's palace

It was in front of this building that tradition has placed the famous episode of *Francis Renouncing his Inheritance and Earthly Possessions,* where he removes his garments and returns them to his father in the presence of the Bishop (as shown in the panel of the *Franciscan legend* in the upper church). At the end of his life, the deathly ill Francis stayed in this building, which has always been considered particularly sacred.

Practically nothing remains of the original room and structure where Francis lived, for it was completely rebuilt in 1612 and then hit by the earthquake of 1832.

Continue to Piazza Garibaldi.

Palazzo Fiumi Roncalli, Confraternity and Oratory of San Francescuccio
(Piazza Garibaldi)

The Palazzo Fiumi Roncalli stands on Piazza Garibaldi. Next to the palazzo is the Oratory of San Leonardo, or of San Francescuccio, renovated in 1428. Frescoes on the facade of the building date to about 1440, with the *Annunciation* and the *Stories of the Pardon*. Of most interest are the *Stories of the Works of Mercy* in monochrome green earth. Practically nothing is known of the artist who painted this cycle in Assisi. It may have been the Umbrian painter Pietro di Giovanni Mazza, or someone more generically known as the "Master of the Works of Mercy". It is one of the best examples of the spread of the International Gothic style in Umbria.

A second, more gifted, artist then painted the famous picture of the *Pardon of Assisi* in the niche which decorates the entrance door. This facade is one of the principal art works of the time, not only in Assisi, but the whole of Umbria.

Inside the Oratory is a cross vaulted nave with frescoes on the walls, including a *Cru-*

◄ Oratory of San Francescuccio

▲ Oratory of San Francescuccio, interior, *Crucifixion*

cifixion and *Saints Leonard and Francis*. Also of interest are the cycles regarding the *Concession of Pardon* by Giuseppe Gislieri and the late 16th century *Stories of Saint Francis*.

Continue along Via Brizi and then Via Bernardo da Quintavalle.

Oratory of San Francesco Piccolino
(vicolo superiore di Sant'Antonio)

A tradition dating to the 15th century (therefore more than two hundred years after the death of Francis, even though the foundation must date at least to the 14th century) indicates this site, originally a stable, as the place where Francis' mother – Monna Pica – came to give birth. The analogy with the stable in Bethlehem and the complete identification of Francis with Christ is evident. In Franciscan mysticism the site thus became the new Bethlehem, while

▼ Oratory of San Francesco Piccolino

the Sacro Convento was the new Jerusalem on Mount Calvary. All of Assisi, like a Sacro Monte of the type spread throughout Tuscany and Italy, could thus repropose the holy places of Palestine.

Chiesa Nuova
(Piazza della Chiesa Nuova)
From the point of view of architecture, this building is one of the most important late Mannerist buildings in Assisi. The paintings too present us with important evidence of the taste of the times, represented by the Giorgetti workshop, the principal one at that time.

The church was dedicated to the followers of Saint Francis, above all those martyred in the name of Christ and the Founder, to celebrate the faith and conversion. This was why a meaningful site for the building was chosen, and the Chiesa Nuova was built on the presumed house where Francis was born, of which the Oratory of San Francesco Piccolino below was also a part.

We know that building was begun in 1615 (so that by 1618 the church must have been on its way to completion), after Brother Alessandro di Trejo, Vicar General of the Observant Franciscan monks, was nominated trustee of the money granted by the patron, Philip III of Spain, to which a plaque still on the facade of the church bears witness. On the broken

◄ Chiesa Nuova

pediment above the entrance is the coat of arms of the Spanish king, while at the sides are, respectively, the emblem of the Franciscans and that of the Vicar General Alessandro di Trejo.

The actual building was co-ordinated by the bishop of the city, Marcello Crescenzi, whose close friendship with the Milanese cardinal Federico Borromeo must be kept in mind. Both of them followed a religious concept that was still closely inspired by the fifteenth century Albertian ideals and forms. Most probably, the model for the building may have come from the Milanese ambience – under the Spanish crown for almost a century. It is therefore no coincidence that, through the Roman Spanish Jesuits to whom the Borromeo were traditionally tied, the plan refers to studies on ancient Roman funerary temples by the Milanese painter and theoretician Giovan Battista Montano in Rome (1608). The drawing for the building was furnished by Fra' Rufino da Cerchiara, but who really designed it remains a moot question.

The brick facade is articulated by four pilaster strips. A cupola rises up over the central part, while small domes over the side arms are hidden by the sloping roofs.

▲ Chiesa Nuova, the high altar

The porch or narthex leads into the church. On the left a small *Chapel of the Relics* or *of the Crucifix* has been fitted into the wall. It is decorated with monochrome paintings of the *Stories of Saint Clare* attributed to Cesare Sermei (1584-1668). On the right, still inside the wall, is the *chapel of San Bernardino*, with monochromes by Sermei of the *Life of the Saint*.

To be noted inside the central space of the church are frescoes dating to c 1620 on the great pylons which support the dome. They depict scenes from the *Life of Saint Francis* and can be attributed to Vincenzo Giorgetti.

The stuccoes date to 1769, although a great deal of renovation and integration was carried out in 1925 (such as the *Evangelists* in the squinches of the dome). A small cell has been cut out of the first pier on the left upon entering, where Pietro Bernardone, Francis' father, shut his son up in an attempt to get him to abandon his ideas of evangelical conversion.

On the left in the great central octagon is the *Chapel of the Immaculate Virgin*, with frescoed scenes on the walls of the *Life of the Virgin* and a fine *Original Sin with Adam and Eve* by Giacomo Giorgetti (1603-1687). The altar painting, the *Madonna with the Cincture*, is by Andrea Polinori (1586-1648), but was not originally painted for this church.

A side door between the Chapel of the Immacolata and the sanctuary leads to the remains of what is traditionally considered the old house of Francis, to which a wall with doors and windows bear witness.

A 17th century tradition says that the chapel opposite the entrance (the main chapel) was Francis' room where he had his *Dream of the palace full of weapons* (shown in scene III in the upper church).

The right arm, or the *Chapel of Sant'Antonio*, is dedicated to the celebration of one of Francis' most important followers, Anthony, who was particularly active in evangelization (a new Saint Paul). The canvas on the altar by Tommaso da Ascoli depicting *Saint Anthony and other Saints* dates to the 18th century. The frescoes on the walls by Vincenzo Giorgetti show more Franciscan martyrs.

From Piazza della Chiesa Nuova continue to Piazza del Comune.

◀ Chiesa Nuova, entrance
to the old house of Saint Francis

▲ ▼ Views of the city

FROM PIAZZA DEL COMUNE TO THE CATHEDRAL OF SAN RUFINO

Piazza del Comune • Temple of Minerva
Palazzo del Capitano del Popolo • Monastery of San Paolo
Palazzo delle Poste • Archaeological Museum • Pinacoteca Civica
Church and convent of Santa Chiara • Cathedral of San Rufino

Piazza del Comune

In 1926 the entire square was redone in an attempt to create a perfect "medieval" setting, radically changing the appearance of the build-

ings. The underlying concept was to make it look as it was when Giotto portrayed it in the scene of *Saint Francis Honored by a Simple Man* in the upper church. In antiquity this area was occupied by a religious complex consisting of the so-called Temple of Minerva and the adjacent porticoed square, with terraces on different levels below as indicated by a study of the center of Assisi. In the early Middle Ages the destruction of the Roman buildings raised the level of the land (circa 5 m) up to that of the upper temple.

Fontana di Piazza (Fountain in the square)

There was a fountain here at least as far back as 1303. The one there now was installed in 1762 (based on the one shown in Cesare Sermei's *Fair of the Pardon in Piazza Maggiore* of 1625 or in Giacomo Lauro's picture of *Assisi* dating to 1599).

The so-called Temple of Minerva and the church of Santa Maria della Minerva

A 16th century tradition identifies the ancient temple which stands on the Piazza del Comune with the cult of Minerva but modern historians believe that it was connected with the cult of Castor and Pollux, together with an ancient spring. This is an extremely well preserved example of Roman religious architecture of the first century BC, the later republican period. The facade has six columns (known therefore as hexastyle) with grooved shafts, originally covered by a thick layer of plaster (still visible in part), which was then painted in bright colors. The capitals are Corinthian, the Attic bases rest on high plinths. A bronze dedication (known as *litterae aeratae*) was set into the entablature.

◄ View of Piazza del Comune

► Fontana di Piazza

At the top is a triangular pediment.

During the Middle Ages the building was the property of the Benedictine monks of Subasio, who ceded it to the City in 1212. It was eventually transformed into a prison, to which the realistic detail of the bars in the scene of *Francis Honored by a Simple Man* in the upper church testifies. Under the pontificate of Pope Callixtus III, in 1456, the ancient Temple was reconsecrated as a church (although work must have been begun when his predecessor, Nicholas V, was pope). Finally in 1539

▼ Piazza del Comune,
the so-called Temple of Minerva

Pope Paul III Farnese had it dedicated to Santa Maria della Minerva.

The cella was lengthened for liturgical reasons by Giacomo Giorgetti in 1634.

The interior is covered by a barrel vault and was frescoed more than a hundred years after Giorgetti's alterations with a *Saint Philip Neri in Glory* and the *Cardinal Virtues* by Francesco Appiani (1704-1792). Whether the barrel vault dates entirely to the 16th century or whether it belongs to an earlier period remains a moot question. The rich altar (with statues of *Purity* and *Chastity* and the image of *God the Father* above center) is in any case by Giorgetti.

▲ Church of Santa Maria della Minerva, high altar

Palazzo del Capitano del Popolo

In 1282 Guidone de' Rossi, Capitano del Popolo, terminated the building of the first Palazzo del Popolo. It was badly damaged in the sack of the city in 1442 (during which most of the area of the Piazza del Comune was destroyed) and was rebuilt in the 16th century. Important fragments of the medieval phase, when the halls were richly decorated with frescoes by the major artists in the city, are now in the Pinacoteca Comunale. Radically restored in 1926, the newly invented Guelph battlements (flat-topped) were added at this time. It has four large round-arched entrances (neo-Romanesque) on the ground floor which lead into rooms decorated in distemper at this time by Adalberto Migliorati.

Palazzo delle Poste (Post Office) and shrine of the *Madonna di Piazza*

The Post Office, built in 1927 by Silvio Gabrielli and Ruggero Antonelli, stands on the western side of the square. It was modeled on the 15th rather than 14th century part of the neighboring

Palazzo dei Priori (in a sort of simplified 'Romanesque'). The site was originally occupied by the Church of San Niccolò (Saint Nicholas).

A fresco with the so-called *Maestà di Piazza* is located in a shrine on the facade of the Palazzo delle Poste. This mural triptych of the *Madonna between Angels and with Saint Francis and Saint Clare Invoking Protection for the City of Assisi* is known to the people as the *Madonna del Popolo*.

The figures of *Saint Francis* and *Saint Bernardino* in the entrance hall of the Palazzo delle Poste were painted in 1927 by Adalberto Migliorati.

Archaeological Museum

In 1926, on the occasion of the *Seventh Centennial of the death of Saint Francis*, it was decided to install the new municipal collection of inscriptions in the former crypt of the church of San Niccolò (in the Piazza del Comune and torn down shortly before). In 1924 the architect

Ruggero Antonelli removed much of the earth fill in the crypt. The premises and itineraries underneath the town square were defined, once the archaeological excavations carried out by the French architect Auguste Pierre Famin in 1836 and continued by Lorenzo Carpinelli had been closed.

A row of columns divides the rectangular cross-vaulted crypt into two aisles. Most of the paving is that of the Roman square.

Of the finds on exhibit in the crypt, the following are of particular note: *sarcophagus decorated with vertical wave motif (strigilated) and with a Bacchic scene at the center; cinerary urn with the depiction of the deceased; nude male statue; boundary stone with inscription in Umbrian; fresco fragments.*

FIRST AND SECOND CORRIDOR. The first corridor leads into the level beneath the Piazza del Comune. To be seen are fragments of the old Roman paving. On the walls are numerous inscriptions, mostly funerary, from Assisi or the surrounding territory.

◀ Archaeological Museum, Roman finds

The second corridor begins after the large *tribunal* (dais) which was situated at the back wall of the square and where the governors sat during ceremonies.

Back to Piazza del Comune. The municipal buildings occupy the south side of the square.

The municipal buildings: the Volta Pinta (Painted Vault), the "Palazzo Nuovo", the Palazzo dei Priori and the Pinacoteca Civica

The entire south wing of the square is taken up by four buildings which were built at various times. They have retained their individual identity even though they became municipal property in the course of the centuries.

The masonry curtain wall is interrupted, at the ground floor level, by the large Volta Pinta, once a passageway that was closed in 1453 and used as a covered market. In 1556 it was decorated with grotesques as well as with other complex allegorical scenes regarding the myths and history of Assisi.

In 1450 work was begun on additions to the Palazzo Nuovo, of which a part dating to the 14th century or earlier had been destroyed in

▼ Piazza del Comune, the south wing

▲ Piazza del Comune, the Volta Pinta (Painted Vault)

1442. At the end of the 15th century Pope Sixtus IV had the architect Baccio Pontelli renovate the whole complex. Then in 1926 it was redone in its original style, with round-arched windows and the application of Pope Sixtus' coat of arms on the facade.

The Palazzo dei Priori was thoroughly restored in 1926 in a neo-fourteenth century style.

The Pinacoteca Civica (Picture Gallery)

In 1926 when the entire complex became municipal property, the new picture gallery was installed on the ground floor of the Palazzo dei Priori to house important works by artists who had worked in the city throughout the centuries. The present arrangement, which separates the archaeological and historical-artistic collections, dates to 1933.

Fragments of the 13th century decoration of the Palazzo del Capitano del Popolo (c 1275) In view of the scarcity of 13th century painting in Assisi, particularly of non-religious subjects, these fragments from the Palazzo Pubblico on the Piazza del Comune, are of particular interest. Shown on the larger pieces are a *procession of knights*, the personification of the *month of October decanting wine into barrels* and that of *November plowing*.

Madonna Enthroned (Maestà) of Giotto's workshop.

This fresco, detached in 1924 for the sake of conservation, also comes from the old Town Hall (later Palazzo del Capitano del Popolo). As early as 1936 Zocca attributed this work to Giotto's workshop, but art historians long remained skeptical. The *Maestà* reflects Giotto's style in his Padua period, in particular regarding the complexity of the spatial layout, and should therefore be dated to shortly before 1305.

Crucifix with the Virgin Mary and Saint John in the side boards, by the Expressionist Master of Santa Chiara (by 1310).

The panel in the shape of a crucifix was painted in tempera by an anonymous master (identified with the Giottesque Expressionist Master), strongly influenced by the conquests of French Angevin painting, in particular the pathos and expressiveness of the faces

Madonna and Child between Saint Francis and Saint Clare by Puccio Capanna (1341).

Our knowledge of the artistic personality of Puccio Capanna is relatively recent and refers to the commission for a fresco, dating to 1341, on the old Porta di San Rufino. This *Madonna* is a precious fragment of this fresco.

Fragment from the confraternity church of San Crispino: the Virgin and Child and the Agony in the Garden (1348-133)

These fragments of important frescoes bear witness to the mid 14th-century phase of Pace di Bartolo's art, when he was more interested in capturing the expressiveness of the features than in a calligraphic flow of line (as in the inner facade of the Chapel of San Giorgio in Santa Chiara).

From Piazza del Comune take Corso Mazzini.

▼ Pinacoteca, Niccolò di Liberatore da Foligno, Standard of the Confraternity of San Crisipino, *The Madonna of Mercy between Saint Francis and Saint Clare*

Piazza Santa Chiara

In 1873 the geometer Attilio Cangi was entrusted with rearranging Piazza Santa Chiara. The 19th century layout with its polygonal fountain continues to provide a spacious panoramic terrace from which the tourist can enjoy fine views of the city and the valley below.

Church and convent of Santa Chiara

The monastery or convent of Santa Chiara with its famous basilica is one of the great poles of Franciscan spirituality in Assisi (the others are the complex of San Francesco and that of Santa Maria degli Angeli). It was built between 1257 and 1265 after Pope Alexander IV had canonized Clare in 1255. The site chosen was that of the old church of San Giorgio, where Francis was originally buried, which gave it a twofold significance, connecting it with the cult of Saint Francis as well as with that of Clare. (All that is left of the original small church is an oratory, not open to the public, in the cloistered zone). This then was where it was decided to bury Clare, making it the pole of devotion to the saint, and ensuring its role as a place particularly dear to Franciscanism. The facade of the church is very sober, although the alternating bands of pink and white stone of Monte Subasio make it particularly pleasing to the eye. The facade, below the tympanum, is divided into two registers by a cornice on brackets. In the lower one, in the center, is a large splayed portal while the one above has a rose window. The triangular tympanum, higher than the actu-

al church, has a small oculus in the center.

The fine rose window consists of four concentric circles, originally with mosaic decoration, and with ninety-six connecting columns that provide a lace-like effect.

The great flying buttresses at the sides together with the cylindrical buttresses set against the walls counteract the thrust of the vaulting, as is the case in the upper church of San Francesco (on the right the flying buttresses have been incorporated into the interior of the convent). It cannot be excluded that both series of buttresses were built around the middle of the 14th century, by the papal legate Gil de Albornoz (un-

▼ Basilica of Santa Chiara

der whose direct control Assisi passed in 1353).

The tallest bell tower in Assisi rises up at the back of the basilica of Santa Chiara. It is divided into four registers, while the cusp is the result of the 1926 restoration in the style of the period.

The interior of the basilica of Santa Chiara consists of a simple nave with four bays, covered with cross vaulting, closed by a transept and terminating in a semicircular apse. The plan is therefore quite like that of the upper church of San Francesco. The semicircular apse is the only thing that distinguishes these two examples in Assisi from the plan adopted in their religious buildings by the Cistercian monks who were followers of Joachim of Fiore in Calabria, and were protected by Frederick II

▼ The complex of Santa Chiara

▲ The convent of Santa Chiara seen from below

and with close ties with Brother Elias.

In Santa Chiara (as in San Francesco) a gallery runs along the interior walls of the basilica, which are now bare. Most of the frescoes which covered them in the 13th and 14th centuries are no longer there and the few remaining fragments, to the left of the entrance, date to 1391. The slender clustered piers set against the wall articulate the space in the nave and the division into bays.

The transept, however, contains an important example of 13th century pictorial decoration, testifying to the activity of masters related first to Giunta Pisano, and then to Giotto, such as Palmerino da Guido, consid-

ered by some to be the Expressionist Master.

The signature of Palmerino di Guido was uncovered when some of the intonaco fell after the earthquake of 1832. In a document drawn up in Bevagna in 1309 Palmerino was indicated as a partner of Giotto. Today opinions vary, ranging from those who identify Palmerino with the Expressionist Master, those who separate the two personalities and those who think the repainting makes it too difficult to judge many of the scenes.

The iconographic program upon which the remaining late 13th century paintings were based begins with the *Stories of the Virgin Mary* (or the *Childhood of Christ*), of *Francis and Clare* (in the

▲ Basilica of Santa Chiara,
external flying buttress

CRYPT. In the third bay, contiguous with the outer walls, are two stairs leading to the crypt that contains the body of Saint Clare, recovered in 1850. The crypt was refurbished between 1851 and 1872 in neo-Gothic style by Giuseppe Morichelli and Francesco Madami, to contain Clare's mortal remains. The paintings are by Madami and Augusto Malatesta. The saint's sarcophagus is located on the second level of the crypt.

CHAPEL OF SAN GIORGIO. Today a glass panel divides the chapel into two different areas for worship: the Oratory of the Crucifix, the first to be encountered after entering the basilica, and the Chapel of the Holy Sacrament.

ORATORIO DEL CROCIFISSO (ORATORY OF THE CRUCIFIX). *Crucifix.* Tradition has it that this is the large *Cross* that was in the half ruined church of San Damiano in 1206, where Francis went every day to pray. The Franciscan tales tell how the painted *Christ* spoke to Francis, converting him completely to Poverty. The date of the Crucifix is open to question. If the traditional tale corresponds to the truth, then the panel, the work of a painter from As-

right transept), moves through the *saints* (in the vaults of the crossing and the apse), and is aimed at presenting the same continuity of the Story of the Church to be found in the Basilica of San Francesco, also reproposing the *Stories of Genesis and the Old Testament* (in the left transept). The loss of the frescoes in the nave unfortunately make it impossible to understand the full didactic value of the narration. Apparently it was a cycle that referred to the life of Saint Clare, with precise theological references (as is the case with the life of Francis in the Franciscan Basilica).

sisi, should date to the middle of the 12th century. On the other hand it is hard to see how such a fine work would have been 'abandoned' in San Damiano. In that case it would fit in more or less with the commissions promoted by the Bishop Clarissimo, who also had the cathedral of San Rufino completely renovated in 1134.

It seems much more likely that this *Crucifix* replaced the one Francis really saw, which must have been more modest. Its identification with that of San Damiano may be due to the fact that in the 13th century it was already thought of as old-fashioned. Christ is shown with his body upright and his eyes wide open, in the h i e r a t i c form of the *Christus triumphans* so typical of Comnene painting in Byzantium which then gave place to the suffering version of Christ in the 13th century provincial Byzantine schools. Frescoes signed by Francesco Tartaglia and dating to 1527, with *Francis Receiving the Stigmata*, the *Madonna Enthroned*, and some *Saints* including *Clare,* are at the side on the right-hand wall of the inner facade.

Across from the altar, behind the cloister grate, are various precious relics: a *breviary*, the *tunic*, the *hood* and a *slipper* belonging to Francis; the *tunic*, the *cloak* and the *hood* belonging to Clare. At one side is a triptych with the *Enthroned Madonna and Child* and, in the shutters, the *Stories of the Childhood and Passion of Christ*, attributed to Rinaldo di Ranuccio, from Spoleto, who painted it around 1270 in a highly composed and delicate style.

◄ Oratory of the Crucifix, *Crucifix of San Damiano*

93

ORATORIO DEL SANTISSIMO SACRAMENTO (ORATORY OF THE HOLY SACRAMENT). The oratory, reserved for prayer alone, also contains fine works of art, exhibited in the space that was renovated in the early 1900s (the faux marble base on the walls was done at the time by Gaetano Brunacci). The fresco fragments on the altar wall date to the 13th and 14th century, while below the lunette on the left wall is a 'mural' polyptych by Puccio Capanna with the *Madonna and Child between Saint Clare, Saint John the Baptist, Saint Michael Archangel* (or *Saint John Evangelist*) *and Saint Francis*. Art historians have related this work with a gift of money (a so-called legacy) of 1335. The painter here was clearly influenced by the art of Simone Martini, but also reveals a certain figural rigidity typical of the Umbrian art world. On the entrance wall, above the doorway, are frescoes by Pace di Bartolo depicting the *Annunciation*, the *Nativity* (or *Manger Scene*), the *Adoration of the Magi, Saint George, the Dragon and the Princess*. These frescoes reveal a peculiar graphic linearity, with highly calligraphic lines, but there are also touches of realism. The scene with *Saint George and the Princess*, in particular, has a typically heraldic feel to it, while the details reveal evident contacts with French miniature painting

▼ Oratory of the Holy Sacrament, Pace di Bartolo, *Nativity*

▲ Oratory of the Holy Sacrament, Pace di Bartolo,
Saint George, the Dragon and the Princess

(see the gown of the *Princess* with its silver buckles). These paintings show Pace di Bartolo – active around the middle of the 14th century – as one of the most significant precursors of Late Gothic style.

CHAPEL OF SANT'AGNESE. On the left side of the hall is the Chapel of Saint Agnes, Clare's sister. She and her sister Beatrice lived together with Clare and the other Franciscan sisters in San Damiano and were originally known as Damianites. The chapel, which contains relics of Saint Agnes and the Blessed Beatrice, was added in the 14th century and is modeled on the chapel of Saint Catherine in the lower church of San Francesco. The square room has a three sided apse at the back and ribbed vaulting. It is difficult to determine the precise date for this chapel, for in the basilica of Santa Chiara the cult of Agnes was already being officiated at the end of the 13th century. This might be still another initiative of Albornoz, after 1353, as the appearance and construction of the room would seem to suggest. Clare's sister was actually named Catherine and it was only after Francis had consecrated her that she changed

her name to Agnes. This would seem to be yet another tie, from the point of view of dedication as well as type, between this chapel and that of Saint Catherine in the lower church. The left vault section of the crossing, closest to the chapel, has an image of *Saint Catherine*.

To be noted is the great care taken in the wall of the apse, where the individual white and pink stones from Subasio have been arranged in a carefully worked out grid pattern. The *Saints* and the *Blessed* in the chapel were painted by Girolamo Marinelli (1595-after 1666) or by Don Sigismondo Spagnoli in 1914, after the frescoes in the transept had been brought back to light.

RIGHT TRANSEPT. The gallery which runs horizontally around the walls of the basilica divides the surface of each wall into two areas which were frescoed by the so-called Expressionist Master (Palmerino di Guido?), a pupil of Giotto, in the first decade of the 14th century. In the upper part, above the gallery, beginning on the left, are the *Last Judgment* and then the *Stories of the Virgin Mary* with the *Annunciation to Joachim*, the *Presentation of the Virgin in the Temple* and the *Marriage of the Vir-*

gin. The part below the gallery is divided into two registers. The upper one contains the *Stories of the Childhood of Christ* with the *Massacre of the Innocents*, the *Flight to Egypt*, *Christ among the Doctors*. In the lower register, on the back wall, are the *Death of Saint Clare* and the *Obsequies of the Saint*. On the altar in the transept is a panel with the *Stories of the Life of Saint Clare* attributed to the so-called Santa Chiara Master or Benvenuto Benvieni and dated in an inscription, to "1283". In the center, in an axial position, is the figure of the *Saint*, as sacral as a Byzantine Madonna, framed by a sort of portico. At the sides the panels with the *Stories*, which frame the figure, should be read from below left upwards and then on the right from top to bottom.

On the left side, from bottom to top: *Clare Receiving the Palm (consecration) from the Bishop of Assisi; Clare is Received by Francis at the Porziuncola; Francis Cuts Clare's hair; Clare Resists the Attempts of Relatives to Take her Back to Assisi, holding on to the altar*. On the right, from the top downwards, beginning under the arch: *Francis Cuts Agnes' Hair* after her *Relatives Attempt to Stop Her from Going into the Convent; Clare and the Miracle of the*

Multiplication of the Loaves for the Hungry Sisters; *The Virgin Mary Appears to the Dying Clare*; the *Funeral Rites of the Saint with Pope Innocent IV and Cardinals Present*. An idea of the qualitative difference is furnished by comparing the anti-naturalistic rendering of depth in the scenes and buildings with their overlapping of figures (parataxis), with Giotto's precise geometric construction of space in the *Franciscan stories*.

CROSSING. The four vault sections of the crossing are dedicated to the *Virgin Mary* and to *Saints* particularly connected to the cult of Saint Clare. In the section towards the apse is a *Madonna and Child* and on the right (the side of the just) *Saint Clare*. Towards the nave are the earlier *Saint Agnes Martyr* and *Saint Agnes of Assisi*, Clare's sister, whose name Francis had changed from Catherine (stressing the identification of the two saints). In the section towards the transept are *Saint Cecilia* and *Saint Lucy*, while in the one towards the left transept, is *Saint Catherine* and *Saint Margaret*.

ALTAR. The altar is set inside a structure (*pergula*) consisting of faceted columns connected by an architrave above, which seems to allude to the screen which separated the liturgical space from that of the pilgrims in medieval churches. The *pergula* was originally medieval but has been frequently restored. It has interesting capitals with plant motifs and human heads.

CRUCIFIX. The famous *Crucifix*, one of the earliest of the 13th century paintings in the Basilica, is set behind the high altar. Generally the

▼ Right transept, Master of Santa Chiara, *Panel of Saint Clare*

work is attributed to the so-called Master of Donna Benedetta (by some considered the early period of the Santa Chiara Master), undoubtedly a follower of Giunta Pisano. Historians therefore believe that the *Crucifix* was done right after 1260, while more recently other art historians have anticipated the date to 1250, referring to the monumental plastic rendering of the forms. Christ is shown as the suffering Christ (*Christus patiens*), his body arched and his eyes closed as in works of the Byzantine provincial schools. At *Christ*'s feet are *Saint Francis* and *Saint Clare* in adoration.

CONCH OF THE APSE. The decoration of the apse conch was done in various phases. A *Blessing Christ* in a tondo is what remains of the 13th – 14th century phase while the style of the Expressionist Master (Palmerino) can be also recognized in the fragmentary scene with the *Annunciation to the Shepherds* in the lower part of the apse (the *flock of sheep*).

The windows in the apse, closed over the centuries, were reopened and redecorated in the course of the restoration carried out for the Franciscan Centennial of 1926.

LEFT TRANSEPT. Two registers with scenes of *Genesis* are in the left transept, on the wall above the gallery. From top to bottom, beginning

◀ Left transept,
Master of the Nativity
of Santa Chiara, *Nativity*

with the right-hand wall, *Creation of the Animals*; *Creation of Man*; *Birth of Eve*; *Original Sin*; *Expulsion from the Garden of Eden*; *Building of the Ark*; *The Flood*; *Fall of the Walls of Jericho*; *Sacrifice of Isaac*. The 'apocalyptic' scenes, such as the *Flood* and the *Fall of Jericho*, are matched in the right transept by the depiction of the *Apocalypse*, an example of precise theological references to relate the various pictures, as in the upper church of San Francesco. The frescoes, which date to the late 13th century, have been attributed to a collaborator of Giotto.

▲ A picturesque lane

On the back wall, in the area below the gallery, is a fresco with the *Nativity* dating to the middle of the 14th century by a painter known as the "Master of the Nativity of Santa Chiara".

Above the altar, on the left, is a panel with an *Enthroned Madonna and Child* known as the *Madonna della Cortina*, probably dating to 1265 on account of the similarities in style with the frescoes in the lower church of San Francesco prior to 1266. In the 18th century this painting was attributed to Benvenuto Benvieni, a painter from Foligno, but art historians now have their doubts. Others have however noted that in style the panel is close both to the *Cross* by the Master of Donna Benedetta, and to works by the so-called "Santa Chiara Master". It has therefore been proposed that this may have been one artist, who worked at length in the pictorial workshop of the basilica.

Upon leaving, move along Via Strati, Via Alessi, Via Dono Doni.

Piazza San Rufino

The square, with the great facade of the cathedral at the back, has a large building on the left side traditionally the house of Saint Clare's parents.

Cathedral of San Rufino
(Piazza San Rufino)

The Cathedral of San Rufino is dedicated to Rufinus, a martyr who was drowned in 238, probably a way of christianizing an ancient cult connected with a spring located on the main terrace of Assisi. As early as the 5th century (tradition says 412) a small votive basilica (more likely a chapel) dedicated to Rufinus was built here, where his relics were kept. His cult was widespread but at the time the cathedral of the city was Santa Maria Maggiore and Rufinus was not yet the patron saint of the city. The small basilica stood on one of the large terraced levels of the Roman settlement (by some it has been identified with the Forum), and traces of a large retaining wall still remain under the floor of the current basilica.

Several hundred years later, in the 11th century when Ugone was bishop, the religious and political life of Assisi changed drastically. In 1036 the basilica was elevated to cathedral and the lower part of the bell tower and the crypt, with fragments of frescoes, still bear witness to the first phase in the construction which transformed the shrine. The facade of the Ugonian cathedral however projected much further out, for the building occupied most of what is now the church square.

Exactly a century later politics changed course and the power of the bishop was reinforced. The Cathedral was once more completely rebuilt and the spacious church square there now was created. In 1134 it was decided to tear down the Ugonian cathedral and the new building was begun in 1140. A plaque walled into the exterior of the apse celebrates the event and the architect, Giovanni da Gubbio. Work went on slowly because of the endless contentions between Guelphs and Ghibellines and in 1212 the area of the sanctuary was finished and the bones of Rufinus were moved there. It was not until 1253 that Pope Innocent IV conse-

► Cathedral of San Rufino

▲ Cathedral of San Rufino,
rose window with symbols of the Evangelists

crated the new basilica, in line with a program of the systematic consecration of the principal basilicas in Assisi.

Once more, as with the Franciscan complex, the patronage of the Emperor Frederick II cannot be excluded for the facade of San Rufino and the rich sculptured decoration of the portals, the loggia and the rose windows. The new facade was modeled on those of the Cathedral and of the church of San Pietro in Spoleto, an imperial city par excellence in Umbria, where the Emperor resided when he was in Central Italy. This would explain why the facade, as indicated by the overlap in masonry, was originally meant to be lower. It was then raised to make room for the great arch in the gable and a fresco or dedicatory mosaic (subsequently either never made or which fell in the course of time).

The lower facade, in white Subasio stone and travertine, is divided into two registers separated by a loggia with columns and round arches, supported by corbel tables decorated with foliage and monstrous figures. The varied sculptural reliefs bear witness to the many changes made in the facade. There is a recessed panel between the central rose window with its three circles of small columns and bands and the loggia. Figures, termed "telamones" or "atlantes" in classical iconography, have been fitted into this space and support the architrave above. Here they are placed on the backs of fantastic animals. *Symbols of the Evangelists* are at the corners of the imaginary square in which the rose window is inscribed, while two other figures were once set in the area between them. The left-hand bracket is now empty, while the one on the right holds a copy added in 1880. At the side of the rose window on the left are two figures of saints while the *Archangel Michael trampling the dragon* is at the center. The main portal is set at the

center of the lowest register, with *lions* on either side, one devouring a man (the "pagan sacrifice") and the other a goat (the "Jewish sacrifice"), to serve as warning to the faithful and keep the Devil at bay. The jambs and architrave of the door are decorated with geometric and plant motifs as well as panels of classical inspiration, while the arch springs from a torus molding with fighting monstrous animals connected with St. John's *Book of the Apocalypse*. On the archivolt the monstrous beings are replaced by groups of uncertain significance. In the lunette is an iconographically significant but rather coarse relief. At the center is a *Blessing God between the moon and the stars*, while on the right is the *Madonna nursing the Infant Jesus* and on the left either *Saint Rufinus* or *Saint John the Evangelist*. Below are three *human heads* whose meaning is still a mystery. Just when the lunette was set there is not known but the ambiguous elements in the *Blessing God* may provide a hint. The figure is crowned like a King and the small mantle he wears is a typically 'terrestrial' dress. The pose is that of Christ Pantocrator (who however generally holds a book in his left hand and raises his right

in the Greek or Latin blessing), used by Frederick II in various images of himself. But it is above all the outstretched hand of this *Blessing God* which brings to mind countless representations of the emperor. Recently iconographic studies of the portal in particular have related it to the theology of Joachim of Fiore, to whom the first Franciscans were particularly drawn through the mediation of Brother Elias, while Frederick II was one of the principal protectors of the Joachimites in Calabria, favoring the convent foundations and the reconstruction of the cathedral of Cosenza.

At the back, on the left, is the bell tower which is generally thought to date to the Ugonian basilica, even though

▼ Cathedral of San Rufino, lion to one side of the portal

Giovanni da Gubbio raised it higher. The oldest bell was cast in 1287. At the base of the bell tower is a vaulted Roman cistern.

Between 1571 and 1585 the interior of the basilica was renovated to plans by Galeazzo Alessi in conformity to the architectural norms dictated by the Council of Trent (although the fact that he died in 1572 makes the actual realization somewhat problematical). The Romanesque church was divided into a nave and two aisles by massive piers, which supported a tall wall with windows (clerestory), while pointed arches joined by open timber roofs, typical of medieval Umbrian churches, covered the side aisles. Alessi profoundly modified the structure of the building, adopting a skilful plan which incorporated the various new principles of worship. The Tridentine norms and the Jesuit places of worship which the architect had in mind (based on a model perfected by Vignola, a friend of his) required churches to have a nave but no aisles, focusing attention on the one altar at the end. There could be chapels dedicated to various saints at the sides, but they were not to disturb the spatial and visual unity of the central hall. The sanctuary was to terminate in a tribune over which there was to be a cupola, as an autonomous space or a new aspect of the old transept. The result was a typically late 16th century plan with the nave joined to an octagonal tribune and a deep monastic choir behind it. Alessi therefore transformed the medieval building into a structure with a great clarity of the surfaces and a precise hierarchy between spaces and furnishings. Some of the altarpieces were done by Dono Doni, such as the *Christ in Glory* (1559), the *Crucifixion* (1563) and the *Deposition from the Cross* (1561), but in the 17th century the definitive installation had not yet been completed and there were as yet no replacements for the medieval decoration and frescoes the new walls concealed. It was only thanks to the commissions of the new bishop, Ludovico Giustiniani (1670), that the altars and furnishings were standardized with Baroque stuccoes and frames.

Inside the Basilica, on either side of the portal and contiguous to the inner facade, are two 19th century statues. On the left is *Saint Francis* (1882) by Giovanni Dupré, a famous Florentine sculptor, while on the left is *Saint Clare* by Giovanni's daughter, Amalia Dupré, also a fine artist.

A door on the left wall leads down to the Roman cistern at the base of the bell tower. The square space is covered by a barrel vault.

Back in the church, 17th century altars line the left wall. The second one was designed in 1664 by Giacomo Giorgetti and has a devotional painting by Francesco Appiani of 1751-1752 , showing the *Intercession of Saints for Assisi* after the earthquake of that year.

The 17th century paintings on the other altars are good examples of the taste of the times in the city, while on the next to the last one is a wooden *Crucifix* dating to 1561.

Under the high altar in the sanctuary (at the center of the tribune), are the remains of Saint Rufinus, while on the altar to the left, dedicated to Saint Rufinus d'Arce, is a canvas of the *Crucifixion* by Dono Doni and his son Lorenzo. The great altarpiece was finished by 1563.

The wooden stalls in the choir date to 1518-1521 and were used by the Chapter celebrants.

In the right arm of the tribune is the altar dedicated to San Vitale, with a painting by Dono and Lorenzo Doni of the *Deposition* or *Lamentation over the Body of Christ*

In the right aisle, on the first altar is a painting by Dono Doni with *Christ in Glory be-*

▼ Cathedral of San Rufino,
Chapel of the Sacrament

tween Saint James, Saint John and, below, *Saints Vitale, Rufinus, Anthony, Clare and Francis*. The painting was finished in 1555, as shown by the date on the frame.

From here one can go to the Cathedral Museum, or, leave the Basilica through the next door and reach Via Dono Doni.

CATHEDRAL MUSEUM AND ORATORY OF SAN FRANCESCO. The cathedral annexes contain premises of considerable interest. The long corridor has fragments of frescoes, part of the medieval decoration of the basilica. In particular to be noted is a *Madonna and Child* attributed to the Expressionist Master of Santa Chiara, while the capitals were part of the Ugonian church. Numerous 17th century canvases (by Giorgetti and Sermei in particular), once in the Cathedral or in other churches in the city, offer yet another important panorama of art in 17th century Assisi.

The museum houses important fragments of 13th century frescoes from the various churches in the city (by the Santa Chiara Master, Puccio Capanna and others).

Of particular note in the first room is the polyptych with the *Madonna Enthroned* and the *Stories of Saint Rufinus* by Nicolò di Liberatore known as L'Alunno. The work comes from the high altar of

▼ Museum, artist unknown, *Saint Francis Consults the Gospel in the church of San Niccolò*

the Cathedral and was painted between 1460 and 1462. In this phase L'Alunno was influenced by Florentine art in the persons of Fra Angelico and Benozzo Gozzoli.

In room two, particular note should be taken of the canvas with *Saint Vitale Restoring the Power of Speech to a Youth* by Cesare Sermei. This painting, dating to the 1630s. Of note in room three is a double-faced standard with the *Martyrdom of Saint Catherine* (on one side) and *Saints James and Anthony Abbot* (on the other) by Orazio Riminaldi.

There is an interesting canvas attributed to Cesare Sermei in the sacristy. It dates to the early decades of the 17th century and shows the *Dying Saint Francis Blessing the City of Assisi*. Originally painted for the bishop's palace, it was then transferred to the cathedral. It should be noted how the Rocca, exaggerated in size, seems to dominate the entire city. From the sacristy one can go to an underground oratory (ORATORY OF SAINT FRANCIS) in which the saint withdrew to pray when he went to the cathedral.

Back in the church, along the right wall (with respect to the main entrance) is the

▲ Museum, Puccio Capanna, *Crucifixion*

Chapel of the Sacrament (Cappella del Sacramento), the most significant example of Baroque art in Assisi by the painter Giovanni Andrea Carloni.

In 1663, subsequent to a bequest in money, the Compagnia del Santissimo Sacramento decided to build a chapel of its own annexed to the Cathedral. The artist and architect Giacomo Giorgetti was entrusted with the undertaking but he was unable to finish the decoration, painting only the *Allegory of Faith* in an oval in the vault. It was probably the new bishop Ludovico Giustiniani (1670) who called in the Genoese painter Giovanni Andrea Carloni, who promised to do the

▲ Cathedral of San Rufino, crypt, sarcophagus of the 3rd cent. AD

rest of the pictorial decoration (although we do not know for sure exactly what is by his hand). His art brought the decorative tastes of Assisi up to date with the new tendencies in Italian art, still subject after all these decades to the influence of the Counter-Reformation. The interior of the chapel is a fine example of the splendor of the Baroque, with polychrome marbles (the altar dates to 1764), gilded angels, painted and illusionistic cornices, canvases with strong chiaroscuro. The depictions include, on the left, *Tobias and the Angel*; *David Receiving the Loaves of the Proposition from Achimelec*; *Sacrifice of Isaac*. On the right: *Hagar in the Desert*; *David Praying for the Plague to Stop*; *Elijah and the Angel*. In the apse: *Nativity of Christ*; *Supper at Emmaus*; *Resurrection*. In the apse conch *Gideon's Victory* and the *Theological Virtues*.

Back in the basilica, near the inner facade is the altar of San Giuseppe, with an altarpiece showing *Saint Joseph Exhibiting the Wedding Ring*. The painting was originally for a processional banner and has been attributed to various artists including Dono Doni, or more recently Berto di Giovanni.

At the back of the nave is the ancient font where Francis, Clare and Agnes were baptized, and, according to legend, the Holy Roman emperor, Frederick II .

CRYPT. To enter the crypt of the Ugonian basilica, uncovered in the excavations of 1895, go out into the square in front of the church, and pass through Ugone's old rectory through a doorway on the right.

Columns, connected by arches which support cross vaulting, divide the crypt into seven small aisles and an apse. The fresco fragments in the apse include a *Saint Costanzo* and the *Symbols of the Evangelists*. The symbols seem to belong to the Ugonian phase of the building when the bishop had the older church rebuilt, between 1028 and 1035.

At the center of the apse is the famous sarcophagus of Saint Rufinus, object of the legendary tug-of-war with sixty men per side to decide whether or not to move the mortal remains of the saint. It is in Luni marble and dates to the Roman period, 3rd century AD, and had apparently been used for the burial of a Roman soldier. The relief on the front narrates the myth of *Selene and Endymion*.

Back in the square, note the **Fountain** abutting the facade of the building on the corner, consisting of a basin divided into seven panels with lion-head decorations. This may be an antique piece reused and set here in 1532.

On the left flank of the Piazza della Cattedrale is Via del Torrione, crossed over by the so-called Arch of the Wind (there are hand-holds to keep one from being blown away by the gusts of the north wind in winter). A few Roman arches are also visible, thought to belong to the old theatre and vaulting which supported the tiers.

Via Perlici starts on the uphill side of the Piazza della Cattedrale. It is a continuation of Via San Rufino.

▼ Piazza San Rufino, fountain

THE FORTRESS ROUTE

Piazza Matteotti (Piazza Nova) • Parco del Pincio
Rocca Minore • Rocca Maggiore

For those who do not feel up to a steep climb, the best thing at this point is to go on to ITINERARY 5.

A walk along the Fortresses does however provide particularly enchanting panoramas and views of Assisi which amply repay one for the fatigue. Those who wish to interrupt this itinerary and go to the next one, must climb the stairs of Vicolo San Lorenzo.

Piazza Matteotti (Piazza Nova)
In Roman times this large space seems to have been the circus, used for chariot races and athletic contests. This entire zone of the old Roman city contained the public buildings concerned with the entertainment of the citizens - the theater, the amphitheater and the circus. A few interesting remains from Roman times are still visible include the central portion, in concrete, of an old patrician tomb on the corner of Via del Torrione, coming from San Rufino. Up to 1597 it was faced with marble slabs, subsequently

▼ Outline of the old Roman amphitheatre

used for the convent of the Capuchin Fathers.

The foundations of the Palazzo Bovi and of the barracks of the Carabinieri rest on remains of the Roman circus and on a large terrace which marked the city limits on this side.

In 1925 the Convitto Nazionale "Principe di Napoli" was built on the square. Post World War II architectural circles and in particular Giovanni Astengo, decried this structure as one of the worst examples of the disfiguring of Assisi in modern times.

Despite all the criticism that has been leveled at the building for over fifty years, it cannot be denied that its mass, with the facade overlooking the square and the tall tower with a roof terrace, does

▲ Piazza Matteotti, remains of a Roman tomb

qualify the piazza, which has been turned into an anonymous parking lot.

From Piazza Matteotti, in the direction of the walls one reaches the so-called Parco del Pincio.

▼ Piazza Matteotti, view of the complex of the Convitto Nazionale "Principe di Napoli"

Parco del Pincio or Public Park
(Via Paul Sabatier)

In Karl Baedeker's famous German guidebook of 1894 on Central Italy – one of the first "travel manuals" in the modern sense – practically no buildings later than the classic period in Assisi are mentioned (nothing on the Franciscan complex, whose works of art were not appreciated by the German lovers of Neo-classicism, except for the new early 19th century crypt). One of the few recent things of note in Assisi and meriting a visit by the foreign traveler (a demonstration of how tourism and its literature follow current fashions) was the Regina Margherita Park known also as "del Pincio". Alfonso

▼ Parco del Pincio, "Antiquities" path

▲ Parco del Pincio, the Greek theatre

Brizi's landscaping of 1882 had aimed at reconstructing the garden of a Roman villa. In the old woods of the Capuchin Convent, Brizi created a series of terraces connected by avenues, and bordered by hedges, which moved up to a pond where, in homage to the Romantic love of landscaped gardens, willows were reflected in the water. The references to antiquity were furnished by Roman columns, ancient entablatures and fragments used as benches, as well as the reconstruction of a small Greek theatre.

In 1921 the Municipal Administration commissioned the Florentine sculptor Giovanni Giovannetti (1884-1930) with the War Monument, in bronze and reused antique travertine.

Back in Piazza Matteotti, take Via Villamena on the north to see the remains of the ancient Roman amphitheatre. Here, as in many other cities (Arles and Florence, for example), medieval houses sprang up along the perimeter, taking advantage of the substructures. The amphitheatre was an elliptical structure with two sets of tiers supported by arcading in concrete and seems to have dated to the 1st century AD.

Along Via Eremo delle Carceri, before reaching the fourteenth century Porta dei Cappuccini, a dirt road runs along the walls up to the Rocca Minore of Assisi.

Rocca Minore or Rocchicciola
The Cassero di Sant'Antonio, known also as Rocca Minore or Rocchicciola, was built by Cardinal Gil de Albornoz to protect the city with a stronghold on the Monte Subasio side. A document of 1365 makes note of the building, and construction may be referred to in a *Diploma* of Frederick II to the City of Assisi dating to 1205, in which fortifications

(more than one) of the city are mentioned.

The remains of a polygonal rampart are in the northwest corner and a few openings furnish a view of a route on a level that is now covered over. The Rocca was probably renovated in line with the newest fortification techniques at the end of the 15th century.

The fortress consists of a barbican and a trapezoidal keep, inside which is the tall tower, on the southeast. The tower is over thirty meters high and divided into three levels, two of which have barrel vaults.

There is also a chapel inside the Rocca. It is known as del Crocifisso (of the Crucifix) and contains a *Crucifixion* with the *Virgin* on the right and *Saint John* on the left, painted by Matteo di Gualdo.

Back in the amphitheatre, continue along Via Perlici up to the 14th century Porta Perlici, before which, on the left, is Via della Rocca which leads to the main fortress of Assisi.

◄ View of the complex of the walls and the Rocca Minore

Rocca Maggiore

From Monte Asio, on which the Rocca Maggiore stands, a splendid panorama can be had of the Umbrian Valley, one of the most enchanting in Central Italy. The Umbrian acropolis, with its sanctuary, seems to have been located on this hill, in proximity to the inhabited center. There is no doubt that there was a fortified site on Monte Asio in antiquity when it was devastated in 545 by Totila, king of the Goths, because it was the headquarters of the Byzantine garrison. The Rocca became part of the imperial

possessions at least as early as 1174, and Frederick Barbarossa stayed there several times after 1177. In 1198, according to tradition, the complex was destroyed by the Guelph population of Assisi in one of the countless struggles between Papacy and Empire, after, again according to tradition, Frederick II had lived there as a child. The tie between the Emperor and Assisi went back to before the fame of Saint Francis, even if much of the story is sur-

▼ The Rocca Maggiore

rounded by legend, to which the tradition that Frederick was baptized in Assisi bears witness.

Almost two centuries after the destruction of the fort in 1198, the legate Gil de Albornoz promoted a program for the fortification of all the principal cities in the Dominion of the Church. The Rocca was restored and fortified in 1365, and incorporated into the property of the Holy See, removing it from the control of the citizens of Assisi.

Albornoz' new building followed its late 12th century imperial antecedent, exploiting the substructures. Between 1394 and 1398 Biordo Michelotti raised the keep, affixing his own emblem on the southern side. Papal control was renewed in the latter half of the 15th century, after decades of in-

▼ The complex of the Rocca Maggiore from the ramparts

ternecine struggles, and a polygonal twelve-sided tower, initially isolated but later attached to the entire complex by walls, was added. It seems to have been begun in 1458 by Jacopo Piccinino son of Niccolò and new Lord of Assisi. Work continued in 1460 and was terminated under Pope Pius II who added his crest after 1464. Probably commissioned by Pope Nicholas V, it is of interest for its specific antiquarian references as well as from the point of view of defensive installations. A central geometric form of this type appealed particularly to Humanist culture in that it was close to the circle, the highest example of perfection.

Between 1535 and 1538 the circular bastion of the Rocca of Assisi was built as protection for the entrance gates. Pope Paul III was at the time promoting adaptations and new fortification structures for the forts of the Papal State, subsequent to a famous survey commissioned from Antonio da Sangallo the Younger. The complex was then used as a prison until it was bought in 1883 by the City. Restoration was begun in 1891 thanks to specialized studies carried out by Alfonso Brizi.

Entrance to the Rocca Maggiore is through a gate next

▲ View of the city walls of the Rocca Maggiore

to Paul III's bastion and under a tower. At the center of the court is the keep and tower, the best defended place for the last desperate defense waiting for aid to come. They both contain several levels meant for the kitchens, lodgings, the room of the lord of the castle and all the service rooms. Marvelous panoramas of Assisi and the valley below as far as Perugia can be had from the top of the keep and from the polygonal tower of "Pius II", which can be reached from the guardwalk along the walls.

Back down from the Rocca, return to a point near the stairs in the Vicolo di San Lorenzo (in conjunction with ITINERARY 3).

FROM THE ROCCA MAGGIORE
TO THE BASILICA OF SAN FRANCESCO

**Seminario Diocesano • Monte Frumentario • Fonte Oliviera
Oratorio dei Pellegrini • Palazzo Giacobetti
Loggia dei Maestri Comacini**

Climb down from the Rocca Maggiore to the stairs of Vicolo di San Lorenzo, where the complex of the Confraternity of San Lorenzo is situated. This is one of the less known parts of Assisi from which particularly enchanting and solitary views can be had.

Arco del Seminario and Seminario Diocesano
(Via del Seminario)
The Seminary arch is what remains of an old gate originally located along the course of the Roman city walls. Beyond the arch is the Seminary building, set into the monastery of Sant'Angelo in Panzo in the 17th century, on the orders of the bishop Marcello Crescenzi. The Seminary arch is therefore also known as "portella di Panzo".

On the other side of the street is the vast former Theological Missionary College, built in 1911 by Attilio Cangi.

Continue along Via San Francesco (the old Via Superba),

▼ The Seminary Arch and the Seminario arcivescovile

▲ Portico of the Monte Frumentario

one of the principal arteries of Assisi and leading directly to the Piazza del Comune. It was transformed in the Baroque period and then was subjected to systematic neo-medieval restoration for the Franciscan year of 1926 (arches and doors were restored and replaced, plaster facing was taken off to reveal the masonry underneath).

Monte Frumentario
(Via San Francesco)
The Portico of Monte Frumentario overlooks the street. This vast structure, originally part of a Hospital founded in 1287, was built over the terracing up to Via Fontebella down below. In the 16th century it was used for selling and storing grain. The portico consists of seven arches which spring from columns with fine carved capitals believed by some to be Byzantine in style (in particular the two on the right, with respect to the entrance). The back wall was completely frescoed with works by the Giottesque Master of Farneto, but only a few fragments are left. Inside, the building still has its original Gothic arches, fine capitals and a few other fresco fragments on the walls.

Fonte Oliviera
(Via San Francesco)
The Oliviera Fount is traditionally attributed to Galeazzo Alessi around 1570.

▲ Fonte Oliviera,
attributed to Galeazzo Alessi

Oratory of the Pellegrini
(Via San Francesco)
This small Oratory was built in 1431 as an annex to the Hospital of the same name and is one of the outstanding elements in the art panorama of Assisi of the latter half of the 15th century. In 1468 Matteo di Pietro, a painter from Gualdo Tadino, worked here. His art is marked by a fusion of late Gothic and Humanist aesthetics. In the 1480s Pierantonio Mezzastris worked there in a style very close to that of L'Alunno, at the time the major master in Assisi. The portal, restored in the 1920s, has portions of frescoes by Matteo di Gualdo above, with *Christ in Glory between Saint Anthony Abbot, Saint James and Music-making Angels*. The pres-

ence of *Saint Anthony* and the *musician angels* stressed the thaumaturgic value of prayer and music, in line with an ancient theory according to which music was particularly useful in healing various diseases (music therapy).
Inside, the altar wall, by Matteo di Gualdo, is articulated by a trompe-l'oeil architecture composed of an architraved portico on which putti are playing. Above is the *Annunciation* while below once more *Musician Angels, Saint James and Saint Anthony*. On the vault and the side walls are frescoes by Pierantonio Mezzastris dating to 1477.

Palazzo Giacobetti (former Breccia Vigilanti) now **Municipal Library**
(Via San Francesco)
The building is an outstanding example of Baroque architecture set into the medieval fabric. The facade, which unifies a series of old buildings, rises up for three floors. It is slightly curved and follows the layout of the street. The portal is framed by two columns in antique marble, while above is the Giacobetti coat of arms.
The rich 17th century pictorial decoration inside was painted for the Breccia-Vigilanti family by various artists. In the *ball room (sa-*

lone delle feste) there is a rich seventeenth century architectural *"quadratura"*(architectural perspective), perhaps by Ventura Salimbeni who also worked for the family in their chapel in Santa Maria degli Angeli.

Loggia dei Maestri Comacini
(Via San Francesco)

The building takes its name from the symbols of the Comacine master masons (from the area around Lake Como) sculptured on the architrave of a doorway together with the date "1485". These symbols – a compass, a rose, a trowel and a square – are those of the Lombard masons who were employed in the construction of the Franciscan complex from its beginnings. The Guild House with its Loggia has often been renovated but the original nucleus probably dates to the 13th century. It was enlarged at the end of the 15th century and work was done on the tower in the early 1900s. Alfonso Brizi was in charge of restoration of the Loggia (1895) and reopened rooms and apertures that had been closed in the course of the centuries, removing, as he said. "the modern plaster, and where necessary plastering so that it resembled the original work".

The steep steps of the Vicolo di Sant'Andrea, adjacent to the Loggia dei Maestri Comacini, leads to a characteristic medieval quarter and the monastery of Sant'Andrea.

▼ The Loggia of the Maestri Comacini

THE FRANCISCAN SHRINES IN THE ENVIRONS OF ASSISI

**Santa Maria degli Angeli • Sanctuary of San Damiano
Pilgrimage church of Santa Maria di Rivotorto • Eremo delle Carceri
Monastery of San Benedetto al Subasio**

There are various important Franciscan sites in the environs of Assisi, a few kilometers from the center. They were chosen by Francis as places of prayer and meditation because at the time they were far from city life, even though today some are real towns which have grown up around the shrines connected with the devotion for the saint.

▼ The pilgrimage church of Santa Maria degli Angeli

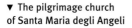

The Pilgrimage Church of Santa Maria degli Angeli or **of the Porziuncola** (hamlet of Santa Maria degli Angeli)

The complex of Santa Maria degli Angeli is located in the valley below Assisi, surrounded by the town of the same name in an area that was still in the midst of swamps in the 13th century . Francis had chosen the site because it was isolated and because there was an old abandoned chapel there, the Porziuncola, with a ceme-

tery that went back to Roman times.

Nowadays nothing remains of that wild and isolated site. Transformation into a congested center, the victim of building speculation, began in the early 1900s after the church had been elevated to the rank of papal basilica and officially inserted into the itinerary of the Franciscan pilgrimages. In the 1920s, on the occasion of the 1926 Centennial of the death of Saint Francis, the expansion of the hamlet of Santa Maria degli Angeli was already beginning to present a real problem from the point of view of town planning. Gustavo Giovannoni attempted to do something about it and suggested that the Gruppo Urbanisti Romani (G.U.R.) prepare a plan, with himself as advisor, for the development of the area. Nothing was ever done with the G.U.R. proposals for Santa Maria degli Angeli (although they were presented in a famous exhibition in Rome in 1930). The same problems of the wildcat growth of towns faced Giovanni Astengo, in the 1950s, but he was no more successful in bringing it to a halt.

The Basilica and the Convent of Santa Maria degli Angeli

The old complex of the Porziuncola was given to Francis by the Benedictine Friars of the monastery of San Bene-

▼ The great square
before the pilgrimage Church

▲ The statue of the Virgin Mary
on the facade of Santa Maria degli Angeli

became Vicar General of the Observant Franciscans, did the zone of Santa Maria degli Angeli stop being primarily a hermitage, as Francis had desired, and became one of the principal centers of the Rule of the Observance and a center of attraction for the faithful. A considerable amount of building followed, sanctioned by a papal decree of 1458. Just what the convent may have looked like between the 14th and 15th centuries is not known, but it certainly had to have a good number of wings, including the so-called "convent of San Bernardino", various chapels some of which incorporated the old "*teghuri*" of the Friars, of which we have information provided by Father Tofi (Fra Stefano da Bettona), in the first half of the 17th century.

To judge from all the images that have come down to us, the church of Santa Maria degli Angeli in Assisi was of a precise type. It was a simple nave (the Porziuncola) with a few autonomous chapels set against it. After the construction of the "long" dormitory in 1492, of a second dormitory in 1527-30 and the infirmary building, in 1558, the complex was completely rearranged. Galeazzo Alessi, an architect from Perugia active at the

detto on Monte Subasio. Subsequently the Franciscans decided to "raise" a house, known as "Casa del Comune" since it stood on public land, behind the Chapel of the Porziuncola, both because their numbers were increasing and because this is where they had begun to hold the Councils of the Order. Any doubts as to the sacredness of Santa Maria degli Angeli soon disappeared, even during Francis' life, when Pope Honorius III conceded indulgence for one day in the year, August 2nd, which became the Feast of the Pardon. Not until Saint Bernardino of Siena

time in Milan, prepared a model for the new church in 1568, but it was held up by the friars of the Convent for almost a year. We know that on March 15, 1569, Jacopo Vignola arrived at the monastery with his "boys" ("*li suoi garzoni*"). Vignola was at the time one of the most important architects working in Rome for the Farnese, a powerful Roman family which had particularly close ties with the Porziuncola. Pope Paul III Farnese had stayed in the complex several times, and had even had a series of rooms known as "del Papa" furnished for him in the old infirmary, later torn down. Vignola remained in Assisi for ten days, until the first stone for the new Santa Maria degli Angeli, approved by Pope

▼ Santa Maria degli Angeli, facade

Pius V Ghislieri, a figure close to the Borromeo in Milan, had been laid. Moreover many construction yard workmen were sent to Assisi from Milan.

The idea of the new imposing pilgrimage church was derived, according to the 16th century sources, from the Casa Santa (house of the Virgin) of Loreto, where the holy building was enclosed within the great basilica. In Assisi however the idea of the old building of the Porziuncola, set at the center of a real Basilica, was to be joined to that of the new reformed churches designed by Vignola, which had altars and autonomous chapels at the sides for private worship.

The fact that Vignola was present when the cornerstone was laid, is usually interpreted as a sign that he was an "advisor" while the absence of Alessi at the ceremony is unusual. We have no idea what Alessi's model was like and what happened to it in the year between its presentation and the beginning of construction, but the fact that Vignola was at the opening ceremony leads one to believe he was directly involved, or at least that there was joint collaboration. Above all it indicates the involvement of the Farnese.

Alessi did not arrive in Assisi until March 1570 to add a new design of the church. When the architect died in 1572, only the foundations of the Basilica had been dug. The terrible earthquake that struck Assisi on January 13, 1832, also shook Santa Maria degli Angeli and after the other tremors of March 13th the facade tilted forwards and the entire vault of the nave and the side aisles fell, while the dome, which rested autonomously on large pylons with a symmetrical distribution of the static stress, remained standing. In August of that year the Vatican Secretariat sent the engineer Luigi Poletti to take measures. By 1840 the restoration was terminated, with all the reconstruction necessary, but the solutions adopted for the facade satisfied no one. In the end the architect entrusted with building the new facade was Cesare Bazzani, although the Soprintendenza ai Monumenti dell'Umbria had expressed numerous reserves. In his initial proposal Bazzani attempted to make the new facade in the spirit of its original times, that is the second half of the 16th century. In search of a sure approval for his project, Bazzani turned to Corrado Ricci, an extremely influential member of the ministerial

commission. His project was finally approved, thanks to his backing in political and religious circles, but not certainly with the enthusiasm of the architectural superintendents. Whatever the case, it had the advantage of definitively finding a remedy for the fragility of the preceding facades by building a powerful volume, and creating proper buttressing for the vaults (in the 1997 earthquake the damages to the basilica were not nearly as serious as those in the quake of 1832). Even though Bazzani did not succeed in having the great fountain and the square in front of the Basilica reorganized as he had planned (the present space was designed by Giuseppe Nicolosi, in 1960), the

▼ Santa Maria degli Angeli, detail of the seventeenth century dome

▲ The Medici Fountain on the left side of the Basilica

entrance, from the exterior, to the Cappella delle Rose, is his. Here he adopted a neo-Gothic style, more in keeping with the taste of 'the time of Francis'.

EXTERIOR. The new facade of the basilica consists of a projecting body in correspondence to the nave and aisles, leaving the space for the side chapels visible. At the top is the large bronze statue of the *Madonna*, dating to 1930, by Guglielmo Colasanti. On the left side of the basilica is the Fonte Medicea, late 16th century, originally at the center of the Piazza and moved here in 1610. The fountain consists of a basin with smooth panels alternating with the coats of arms of the Florentine family, and of a

surround where the emblems alternate with shields (clipei), separated by large brackets.

INTERIOR. The interior has a nave and two aisles, flanked by side chapels, separated by Doric piers. The wide nave is covered by a large barrel vault, while the side aisles have cross vaulting. Below the large dome set over the sanctuary is the Porziuncola, the small building that was incorporated into the interior of the new basilica in the 16th century. In the side chapels, acquired and decorated by individual noble families in the early 17th century, are some of the most important examples of late Mannerist painting in Umbria and the later periods up to the 18th century.

RIGHT AISLE. Near the inner facade is the Chapel of Saint Anthony Abbot, with an altarpiece of the *Saint* painted by Giacomo Giorgetti in 1670. To be noted on the vault is *Saint Anthony in Glory* and in the roundels the allegories of *Prudence, Justice, Fortitude* and *Temperance* by Francesco Appiani, of 1756.

Then comes the Chapel of Saint John the Baptist, which was decorated in 1602 by Cesare Sermei, with *Stories of the Saint.*

Next is the Chapel of Saint Anne, of the Fiumi-Roncalli family, who owned the palazzo of the same name in the city. The paintings were commissioned from Cristoforo Roncalli and Antonio Circignani known as Pomarancio,

in 1602-1603, with scenes of the *Life of the Virgin.*

The next chapel is dedicated to Pope Pius V, who supported Alessi's renewal of the basilica. Between 1602 and 1603 the Bolognese painter Baldassarre Croce painted scenes from the *Life and Miracles of Saint Francis* on the right and left walls, while the 18th century altarpiece depicts the *Ecstasy of Saint Pius V.*

The last is the Chapel of the Annunciation, or Pontani-Coli from the name of the Perugian family which bought it in 1591 and then commissioned Federico Barocci to paint the famous altarpiece now in the Basilica Museum

▼ Santa Maria degli Angeli, interior

in 1596. To be noted are the frescoes on the walls, with scenes of the *Life of Saint Francis* by Silla Piccinini (1585-1600). Attention should be paid in particular to the *Procession of the Pardon of Assisi*, where the basilica of Santa Maria degli Angeli can be seen practically terminated. The frescoes have been attributed to Piccinini on stylistic grounds. The detail of the finished dome (despite the difficulties involved in building it) and the scene of the two women below left however lead one to think it is much later than 1600.

RIGHT TRANSEPT. Three chapels have been fitted into this space. To be noted in the right-hand chapel (of San Pietro d'Alcántara) is the early 15th century statue on the altar of the *Madonna del Latte (Nursing Madonna)*, while in the central chapel (of San Pietro in Vincoli) the great Baroque altar dating to 1675 has stuccoes done by a pupil of Bernini.

From the arm of the transept access is to the area of the sanctuary.

SANCTUARY. The tall dome supported by four powerful triangular pylons is set over the sanctuary. The basic idea is generally attributed to Alessi, but the great dome was built almost two centuries after his death with a whole series of modifications which make it a product of 17th century engineering. Nineteenth century canvases by Stefano Montanari of Rimini illustrating *Stories* connected with the *Feast of the Pardon* decorate the lower part of the sanctuary while the scenes of Franciscan episodes that took place in Santa Maria degli Angeli were painted by Francesco Appiani in the pendentives in 1757. The great carved choir stalls that close this area date to the 17th century. At the center of the sanctuary, under the great dome, is the Chapel of the Porziuncola.

THE PORZIUNCOLA. It is hard to imagine what the Porziuncola was like when Francis received it as a gift from the Benedictine monks of Monte Subasio, for the building has been changed so often in the course of the centuries. We know only that the original chapel was a tiny church. It is now in the form of a simple room, not much more than nine meters long and about four meters wide, in stone and with a gabled roof (the shrine at the top was set up after the earthquake of 1832). On the north is a semicircular apse, frequently rebuilt, while on the south, opposite the main entrance to the basili-

▲ The Porziuncola, main facade

ca, is a large round-arched aperture, the result of an enlargement. Inside, the chapel is covered by a stone barrel vault, in the shape of a Gothic arch in cross section. The latest studies (Romanini) confirm the antiquity of the Porziuncola as we see it today, chronologically set between the late 12th and early 13th century. On the outer facade is a fresco painted in 1839 by the Nazarene painter Johann Friedrich Overbeck, with *Saint Francis Kneeling at the Feet of Christ and the Virgin* (the so-called *Pardon of Assisi*).

▼ The Porziuncola, the exterior of the apse

The fresco of the *Crucifixion* on the apse wall is particularly famous. The detachment of repainted intonaco fragments in the recent quake of 1997 more clearly revealed the original parts by Pietro Perugino, who worked with Andrea d'Assisi known as L'Ingegno (which explains the varying attributions). Vasari mentioned the work too, informed by a document of 1486 relating to its commission. It is a relatively large fresco, solemn in its composition. The three *crosses* are silhouetted on Mount Calvary while the *horsemen* all around recall the scene painted by Pietro Lorenzetti in the lower church of San Francesco, although Perugino added a typically humanist approach, particularly attentive to the expressions and the details of the clothing. The fresco was partially destroyed when the large new basilica was built in the 16th century. In 1832 in view of the importance of the work and its precarious state of preservation, the painter Francesco Cappelletti decided to "touch it up" with extensive repainting retaining the 15th century layout and a small fragment of the original. Although his additions destroyed the legibility of the original, they did preserve its appearance, which came to light when they fell

off. In 1974 an *Annunciation* was detached from beneath the intonaco of Perugino's fresco, a demonstration of the numerous phases and frequent renovations of this important site of worship. Repeated earthquakes have taken their toll of the decorations inside the Porziuncola and all that remains are a few faces of *Saints* and *Apostles*.

The large panel over the altar, divided into compartments and dating to 1393, was commissioned from Ilario da Viterbo to fulfill a vow made by Francesco da Sangemini. Ilario worked at length in the construction yard of the Cathedral of Orvi-

▼ Interior of the apse of the Porziuncola

eto and his partiality for architectural spaces and perspective views, close to the styles of the Northern painters, is accentuated here. The panel has recently been restored bringing to light its brilliant colors, even if the paint itself is dotted with countless small bruises. It was indeed the custom for pilgrims who visited the Porziuncola to throw coins against this panel as offerings. There is an *Annunciation* at the center of the altarpiece while of note among the various scenes are *Saint Francis Announcing the Granting of the Indulgence for Those who Visit the Porziuncola for the Feast of the Pardon* and *Saint Francis Throwing Himself into the Briars to Resist the Temptations of the Devil*. Above are *Christ and the Virgin Appearing to Francis*, a key episode in Franciscan devotion in the pilgrimage church of Santa Maria degli Angeli.

The recent restorations subsequent to the 1997 earthquake have shown the Porziuncola as the great extraordinary reliquary that it is. After cleaning, the gabled roof has completely changed aspect. The centuries of layers of fixatives and dust have given way to two levels of Subasiao stone with white and red inlays, Marian stars and diamonds, so that the building now looks like a precious jewel box. The dark grotto, all in stone, we were used to seeing, reflected the neo-medieval nineteenth century taste: its walls were actually entirely frescoed and the roof inlayed in brilliant colors.

CAPPELLA DEL TRANSITO. The first document in which reference to the chapel is found dates to 1334, but this space, where Francis drew his last breath, must originally have been part of the Franciscan infirmary. Subsequently it was transformed into an oratory and then, in the course of the centuries, was transformed with the addition of a choir, or a sacristy which seems to have served both the Porziuncola and this chapel.

This place of worship now consists of a single room built in stone, which is rectangular externally, but almost octagonal inside.

On the outer walls are 19th century frescoes by Domenico Bruschi (1886) with the *Death of Saint Francis* or the *Death and Funeral Rites of the Saint*. The frescoes inside of 1514-1520 c. are by Giovanni di Pietro known as lo Spagna, and depict Francis' first *Companions* and the first Franciscan *Saints* and *Martyrs*. Even though they have been con-

siderably repainted, they still show that lo Spagna had overcome that somber sentimentalism which had characterized the works of Perugino's other followers. Here the faces of the *Saints* are relaxed and radiant, related to the art of Raphael. The glazed statue of *Saint Francis* behind the altar is by Andrea della Robbia and dates to 1490. A case contains the cord, or cincture, of the saint.

In the corridor that leads to the crypt, the famous canvas with the *Annunciation,* painted by Federico Barocci in 1596, is hung over the door. Here the painter from Urbino reveals his inventiveness in that fresh and refined figurative color that was so greatly appreciated in central Italy around the turn of the 16th century.

▼ Chapel of the Transito

▲ Chapel of the Transito,
reliquary with the Holy Cincture

CRYPT. Entrance to the crypt is from the sanctuary. It was dug in 1968 to designs by Bruno Apollonj-Ghetti so that the remains of the "Casa del Comune" could be seen.

This was the building which Francis had begun to tear down but which he then had to leave because it was public property. The altar in the crypt is a tree-trunk shaped sculpture by Francesco Prosperi (1906-1973).

SACRISTY. The frescoes in the lunettes of this large space covered by a pavilion vault are by Gerolamo Martelli and show *Franciscan saints* and *Stories of Saint Francis*. The wardrobes along the walls date to the 17th century.

From here one can go to the sacred spaces of the Convent passing through the "bed of thornless roses", where, according to tradition, Francis threw himself to resist being tempted by the Devil and where he had the vision of Mary and Christ. Next to it is the Cappella delle Rose or Chapel of the Roses.

CAPPELLA DELLE ROSE. There are two parts to this chapel. The inner part, enlarged and rebuilt in 1344, stood on the site of the "*teghurio*", the brushwood hut where Saint Francis lived. The front part, the Oratory, was built by San

◄ Chapel of the Transito,
Giovanni Spagna, *Saints Anthony, Bonaventure and Berardo*

Bernardino of Siena at the beginning of the 15th century. On the walls are important frescoes by Tiberio d'Assisi with *Stories of the life of Saint Francis*. In particular to be noted: *Saint Francis Throwing Himself into the Briars; Angels Lead the Saint to the Porziuncola; Francis Invoking Pardon; Confirmation by Pope Honorius IV; the Publication of the Indulgence; Saint Francis with Eleven Companions; Saints Bonaventure, Louis, Anthony of Padua, Clare and Elisabeth.*

The artist worked on these frescoes in two different periods. In 1509 he did the figures of *Francis with his First Followers* and then, in 1516, he was entrusted with the episodes of the life of the saint. Nothing is signed so that attribution to Tiberio is on stylistic grounds. Art historians are practically unanimous in assigning the frescoes to him, but they disagree as to their quality, with judgments ranging from "excellent" to "weak and lacking in accuracy".

After visiting the Cappella del Pianto (Chapel of Tears, restored in 1926) and seeing the remains of the old convent, begun in 1230 and enlarged in 1288, the Museum of the Basilica can be visited.

▼ Andrea della Robbia, altar frontal in glazed terracotta with the *Coronation of the Virgin* at the center

MUSEUM OF SANTA MARIA DEGLI ANGELI. Just a few of the truly fine works of art to be found in the museum can be mentioned here. These include in Room Two, the famous *Crucifix* painted by Giunta Pisano in 1236, one of the first examples in the west of the Byzantine iconography of the *Christo patiens*, the panel of *Saint Francis*, by the Saint Francis Master and on which, according to tradition, the body of the Saint was laid the day after his death; the panel with *Saint Francis* attributed to Cimabue (but more probably a later copy).

In Room Three is a bas-relief by Libero Andreotti, of the early 1900s.

CONVENTINO. The premises of the Conventino were begun in 1493 when the monastic structures became too crowded. The lunettes in the cloister were decorated in 1666 with *Stories of Saint Francis* by Francesco Providoni, a painter from Bologna, who also did the famous reconstruction of the original appearance of the Porziuncola ('original' on the basis of what the 13th century sources filtered through 17th century taste provided). To be noted in the Refectory is a *Crucifixion* by Dono Doni. The same person who commissioned this fresco from Doni in 1561 also commissioned the construction of the large Refectory, begun in 1559. The painting is mentioned by Vasari, who saw it in 1563, when Doni had already finished other works in the convent begun by Lo Spagna in 1541, but then destroyed when the Alessian basilica was built. This *Crucifixion* is the only part of Doni's cycle still extant. Michelangelo's style via Vasari's influence is particularly relevant here.

Back in the basilica, in the sanctuary area, the visit moves on to the left part.

▶ Museum,
Giunta Pisano,
Crucifix

ORATORY OF THE SACRA-MENT. This space was turned into a place for meditation and prayer in 1984 and has various works of interest on the walls. On the right is a canvas with *Saint Peter of Alcántara* by Giacomo Giorgetti. Of particular note are the fragments of an *Annunciation* (the *Angel* and *Mary*) by Pietro Perugino on the back wall on either side of the altar. They were detached from the apse of the Porziuncola in 1830 and then considerably repainted by Luigi Castelletti.

LEFT ARM OF THE TRANSEPT. The Chapel of Saint Anthony of Padua is located at the head of the transept, with a wooden carved and painted *Crucifix* on the altar. It dates to the early 16th century and is of Nordic school.

LEFT AISLE. Contiguous to the left arm of the transept is the chapel of the Rosary, decorated between 1659 and 1715 by Carlo Morelli, a painter from Assisi. To be noted on the right wall *Galeazzo Alessi Presenting the Project for the New Basilica of Santa Maria degli Angeli to Pope Pius V*, painted either by a pupil of the school of Conca, or by Baldassarre Orsini (1732-1810).
Then comes the Chapel of the Coronation of the Virgin,

frescoed in 1603 by Simone Ciburri. It is interesting that the *Saint Diego Healing the Son of the King of Spain* was painted on the left wall of this chapel, stressing the bonds of the Franciscan family with the Spanish rulers, more or less in the same period in which the Chiesa Nuova, paid for by the King of Spain, Philip III, was being planned.
Next is the Chapel of the Deposition of the Lord. It belongs to the Vigilanti family of Assisi, who owned the

▼ Museum, Saint Francis Master,
Saint Francis panel

palazzo of the same name in the city, which then passed to Giacobetti and is now the Municipal Library. The decoration of the chapel was entrusted in 1603 to Ventura Salimbeni, a painter from Siena who had also been commissioned by the Breccia-Viginati family for work in the ball room in their city residence. Baldassare Croce from Bologna and Piergirolamo Crispolti also worked in the chapel.

The next chapel is dedicated to the Stigmata of Saint Francis. Around 1630 Cesare Sermei and Giacomo Giorgetti, the major painters of this time in Assisi, worked there.

The last chapel in the aisle, contiguous to the inner facade, is the one dedicated to Saint Diego d'Alcalà, frescoed in the 18th century by Benedetto and Giovanni Cavallucci, Baldassare Orsini and Anton Maria Garbi, with *Stories of the Saint and the Pardon of Assisi*.

The Sanctuary of San Damiano

About a kilometer and a half from Assisi, southeast from the Porta Nuova near the monastery of Santa Chiara, is the complex of San Damiano, where Francis heard the voice of God come to him from the old *Crucifix* (now in Santa Chiara) urging his conversion (1205 or 1206). The old chapel was

▼ The Sanctuary of San Damiano, entrance

restored by Francis and this is where Clare and her first companions (known therefore as Damianites) stayed until 1253 when Clare died. Her followers then moved to the convent in the city in 1260, leaving San Damiano to the Franciscan friars. The holy places are therefore bound both to Francis, who is said to have composed part of his *Canticle of the Creatures* here, and to Saint Clare.

We know that a small church was erected in honor of Saint Damian between the 8th and 9th century, with next to it a hostel for pilgrims on their way to Rome. The Benedictine priory is already attested to in 1030. In Francis' time however the place had fallen into ruin and the only one living there was a humble priest, Pietro. After the revelation, Francis decided to go back and live there with a small community of followers and they restored the complex before turning it over to Clare and her community. Something of particular importance happened here in 1240, which has traditionally been interpreted as a miracle. After being excommunicated, Frederick II sent troops to take over control of the city, knowing he could count on the backing of many of Francis' followers and hoping that Clare too would sup-

▼ San Damiano, the cloister

◄ San Damiano, apse of the church, *Madonna and Child*

port him. In his *Legend of Saint Clare*, Thomas of Celano stresses the fact that the emperor's troops were composed mainly of Saracen infidels and that they came intending to plunder the city. Clare showed them the

tabernacle of the Eucharist and miraculously put them to flight.

The church square of San Damiano is bordered on three sides by a portico with segmental arches (a sort of external cloister). The facade of the small church behind is gabled and built of irregular stone masonry. The way in which the arches of the portico cut into the oculus on the facade reveals differences in level in the original building. The shrine on the right of the small square is decorated with a mid-14th century fresco of a *Madonna and Child between Saint Clare and Saint Francis and a Worshipper* assigned to the San Crispino Master. On the right, is the entrance to the church chapels, initially the rectory.

▼ San Damiano, Chapel of San Girolamo, Tiberio d'Assisi, *Virgin Enthroned with Saints*

▲ San Damiano, refectory

There are frescoes of 1517 in the chapel of Saint Jerome. The lunette on the back wall has the *Virgin Enthroned between Saints Francis, Clare, Bernardino and Jerome.* The style is clearly that of Tiberio d'Assisi who, especially in S*aint Clare*, repeats the image he had already done in the Chapel of the Roses in Santa Maria degli Angeli, greatly influenced by Simone Martini. The figures of *Saints Sebastian* and *Roch* on the left wall are considered Tiberio's last works and are dated to 1522.

Entry to the church is through the Chapel of the Crucifix (1555), with a wooden *Crucifix* of 1637 that is highly expressionistic. The church interior is a simple nave with a pointed vault. The sanctuary area, with considerably lower vaulting, was probably once a crypt, while the sanctuary originally seems to have been raised and corresponded to what is now the Oratory of Saint Clare. There is a small window near the main entrance, on the right wall, from which Francis is supposed to have thrown a purse full of money. All around are fragments of early 14th century frescoes which recall the episode.

The *Crucifix* on high on the central arch, before the sanctuary, is a modern copy of the one which miraculously spoke to Saint Francis and which is now in Santa Chiara. In the apse is a

Madonna and Child between Saints Rufinus and Damian assigned to the Master of Farneto, of the early 14th century. The wooden choir stalls date to 1504.

Entrance on the right of the hall is to the "Coretto di Santa Chiara" where the first Damianites gathered in prayer with Clare (the simple stalls stress their rule of Poverty) and, on the back wall, a *Crucifixion* by Pierantonio Mezzastris of 1482. From here steps lead up, next to Saint Clare's garden, to the saint's oratory. This simple room, where Clare privately prayed daily, was decorated in the 14th century with frescoes which have however been considerably overpainted.

Further up is the bare dormitory of the Damianites. On the left wall a *Cross* marks the place where Clare died on August 11, 1253.

Next to the church is the convent cloister with various frescoes on the walls, including *Saint Francis Receiving the Stigmata* and the *Annunciation* by Eusebio da San Giorgio. The pictures, set respectively on the left and right walls of the entrance, inside painted compartments, are signed and dated "1507". On one side of the cloister is the refectory , with 17th century frescoes by Cesare Sermei.

Church of Santa Maria di Rivotorto

As one of the first places in which the saint and his first followers lived (apparently between 1208 and 1209), the locality of Rivotorto was important in the life of Saint Francis. It was from here that they went to Rome to ask for the first approval of the Rule, and then it was to here that they returned.

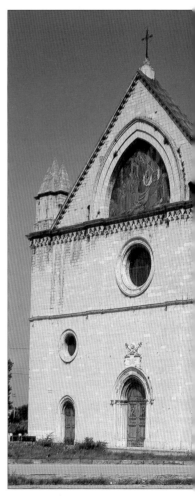

While the exact location of Rivotorto has not been identified, in the 15th century this is given as the traditional site. The building of a real church in place of the original chapel dates to 1455, while the larger church begun by Pope Sixtus V in 1568 was finished in 1640. It was however Pope Benedict XIV (1740-1758) who raised its status to that of a papal basilica, official recognition of its importance. After the earthquake of 1852 it was decided to radically restore the building, in keeping with the revival of the Franciscan cult, the result of the discovery of the mortal remains of the saint. Assisi scholars insist that the Franciscan site

▼ The pilgrimage church of Rivotorto

▲ Rivotorto, entrance to the hovel

of Rivotorto is here, where this pilgrimage church now stands and many art historians have accepted this identification. Until the middle of the 15th century the swamps which covered the plain of Assisi reached up to here, and it seems quite plausible that a community which desired to live in isolation like the first Franciscans should have settled here.

The reconstruction of 1853, promoted by Fra Bernardo Tini, intended to repropose the appearance of the principal religious buildings in 13th century Assisi. The main facade was modeled on the cathedral of San Rufino, while the basilica of Santa Chiara with its buttresses was taken as model for the side. Note the steep triangular pediment which crowns the facade in Rivotorto, with an arch at the center which

◄ Rivotorto, interior of the hovel

▲ Rivotorto, bas-reliefs in the hovel of Saint Francis

contains a mosaic done in 1955 (missing or detached in San Rufino). Note also the division into two horizontal registers with the hierarchy between the rose windows and the vertical pilasters which echo the division of the inner spaces.

In 1926 a *teghurio*, or hovel, was reconstructed in the nave. It is composed of three rooms, *Saint Francis' bed,* the *chapel* and the *kitchen*. What we have here is the reproduction of a place, with its bare simplicity, that was very dear to the Franciscan mysticism so fashionable in the early 1900s. The series of canvases by Cesare Sermei (1640) which decorated the 16th century church recalled the early episodes of the life of the Franciscan community, with *Saint Francis Abandoning the Hovel for the Porziuncola (later Santa Maria degli Angeli)*. The fact that Francis abandoned the site because of the hostility of a local peasant, who considered the first Franciscans mad vagabonds, is also one of the reasons why the precise location was soon forgotten.

The Eremo delle Carceri or Forest Hermitage

A road leads from the Porta dei Cappuccini, in the northern part of the city below the Rocca Minore, to Monte Subasio and the Eremo delle Carceri, in an impervious secluded site in the midst of the forest where Francis and his followers withdrew in complete solitude inside

▲ ▼ The isolated site of the Eremo delle Carceri and a view of the complex

natural grottoes in the rock. A community of hermits lived here back in the early times of Christianity, and the Franciscan settlement wanted to renew the immediacy and purity of the first message of the Gospels. The name "prisons" was then given to these premises, typical of the most austere eastern coenobitic colleges, with the extreme poverty and isolation of a prison. Medieval traditions regard-

ing the life of Francis also say that it was here that he "imprisoned himself". In the 14th century the site was already the symbol of the purity of Franciscan teaching compared with the opulence of the Franciscan complex in Assisi. It was then that the small church dedicated to the Madonna was built next to the tiny Oratory where Francis and his followers used to gather. The place was then enlarged and refurbished by San Bernardino of Siena, the famous 15th century preacher of the Observance.

Entrance to the complex is from a small terrace, known as Chiostrino dei Frati or Friars' Small Cloister, overlooking the valley below. The so-called "Well of Saint Francis" is in the cloister.

▼ Eremo delle Carceri, the panoramic terrace overlooking the valley

▲ Eremo delle Carceri, Oratory of San Bernardino

The entrance to the Oratory of San Bernardino, a small vaulted room, with an early 15th century *Crucifixion*, is under a shed roof. On the altar in the Chapel of Santa Maria delle Carceri is a *Madonna and Child with Saint Francis* by Tiberio d'Assisi, of 1506. Further down is the Grotto of Saint Francis, where the saint used to rest on a bed cut into the rock with a log as his pillow when he was in the hermitage.

Outside towards the woods behind, near the exit from the sanctuary, there is a slab in the floor, with a hole in it. Tradition says the Devil fled through this hole after having tempted Francis and been driven away by Brother Rufino. In the woods there are examples of the so-called 'diffused monastery' typical of the hermit. An example of a single chapel is the Chapel of the Magdalene, with the mortal remains of the blessed Barnaba Manassei of Terni, who died in 1477. Manassei invented the Monti di Pietà, those financial institutions which made it possible for all the Christians who had loaned money to avoid the accusation of usury for they were controlled by the Church. In the West this function was covered by the Jews.

A walk along the so-called Viale di San Francesco in the midst of the woods takes one to the caves which were used by the early hermits and by Francis' companions when they withdrew in prayer.

Monastery of San Benedetto al Subasio

The Abbey of San Benedetto is situated on Monte Subasio, at an altitude of 700 meters. The Benedictine monks who lived here were the ones who gave Francis the Porziuncola, later Santa Maria degli Angeli. In the 13th century the so-called Temple of Minerva, in the Piazza Comunale in Assisi, also belonged to this powerful monastery.

The complex, founded before 1051, was destroyed in 1399 by the City of Assisi because it was the refuge of rebels. Restoration began in 1945. The abbey church, characterized by an Egyptian type plan (in tau form) like that then adopted by the Franciscan Order, has been rebuilt. It is likely that the building was renovated in the 13th century, while the crypt below, divided into five aisles by eight columns with leaf capitals, belongs to an earlier phase. In another wing of the complex there is a second crypt, perhaps from the 7th or 8th century, with three imposing columns.

▼ Monastery of San Benedetto al Subasio

PRACTICAL INFORMATION

NOTE

The addresses and items listed have been freely chosen by the editors. This by no means implies that whoever or whatever is not listed is in any way not up to the same standards.

HOW TO GET THERE

BY CAR

Autostrada A14 Adriatica:
- Cesena exit (150 km from Assisi), continue towards Perugia (E 45) up to exit for Assisi Civitanova Marche exit, continue along the Foligno-Peruga route to the exit for Assisi Autostrada A 1 del Sole:
- Valdichiana exit to Perugia and then continue towards Cesena (E 45) up to the Assisi exit
- Orte exit and continue to Peruga-Cesena (E 45) up to the Assisi exit

BY TRAIN

Florence-Terontola-Perugia-Foligno line (Station of Assisi/S.Maria degli Angeli)

BY AIR

The Airport of Umbria (località S. Egidio, 13 km from Assisi) is connected with regular flights to Bologna and Milan

USEFUL NUMBERS

Town Hall ☎ 075 81381
Carabinieri ☎ 075 812376-812239
State Police ☎ 075 819091
Fire Department ☎ 075 812222
Municipal Police ☎ 075 8138284
First Aid ☎ 075 839227
Ambulances ☎ 118 - 075 812824
Red Cross ☎ 075 8043059
Doctors on call ☎ 075 8139517
Hospital ☎ 075 81391
Pharmacy ☎ 075 8139224
Post Office ☎ 075 812355
Taxi ☎ 075 813193
Regional Umbrian Airport Sant'Egidio ☎ 075 592141
Azienda Perugina della Mobilità ☎ 075 5067894 - N. Verde 800 512141

MUSEUMS

Roman Forum and Archaeological Collection
Via Portica - ☎ 075 813053
🕐 From Sept. 26 to Mar. 15
   10 AM-1 PM/2-5 PM
   From Mar. 16 – Sept. 25
   10 AM -1 PM/3-7 PM

Pinacoteca - Piazza del Comune, 1
☎ 075 812579
🕐 From Sept. 26 to Mar. 15
   10 AM-1 PM/2-5 PM
   From Mar. 16 – Sept. 25
   10 AM -1 PM/3-7 PM

Rocca Maggiore ☎ 075 815292
🕐 From 10 to sunset

HOTELS

ASSISI

**** Grand Hotel Assisi
Via Fratelli Canonichetti
☎ 075 81501 🖷 075 8150777
**** Subasio - Via Frate Elia, 2
☎ 075 812206 🖷 075 816691
*** Dei Priori - Corso Mazzini, 15
☎ 075 812237 🖷 075 816804
*** Fontebella - Via Fontebella, 25
☎ 075 812883 🖷 075 812941
*** Giotto - Via Fontebella, 41
☎ 075 812209 🖷 075 816479
*** Hermitage - Via degli Aromatari, 1
☎ 075 812764 🖷 075 816691
*** Il Castello - Viale Marconi, 1B
☎ 075 813683 🖷 075 812567
*** La Terrazza - Via F.lli Canonichetti
Loc. S. Potente
☎ 075 812368 🖷 075 816142
*** Porta Nuova - Viale Umberto I, 21
☎ 075 812405 🖷 075 816539
*** San Francesco - Via S. Francesco, 48
☎ 075 812281 🖷 075 816237
*** San Pietro - Piazza S. Pietro, 5
☎ 075 812452 🖷 075 816332
*** Umbra - Via degli Archi, 6
☎ 075 812240 🖷 075 813653

*** **Viole** - Via Assisana, 67 - Loc. Viole
☎ 075 8065409 🖷 075 8064635
*** **Windsor Savoia** - Viale Marconi, 1
☎ 075 812210 🖷 075 813659
** **Alexander** - Piazzetta Chiesa Nuova, 6
☎ 075 816190 🖷 075 816190
** **Ancajani** - Via Ancajani, 16
☎ 075 815128 🖷 075 815129
** **Ascesi** - Via Frate Elia, 5
☎ 075 812420 🖷 075 812420
** **Belvedere** - Via Borgo Aretino, 13
☎ 075 812460 🖷 075 816812
** **Berti** - Piazza S. Pietro, 24
☎ 075 813466 🖷 075 816870
** **Country House** - Via di Valecchie, 118
☎ 075 816363 🖷 075 816363
** **Da Angelo** - Loc. S. Potente, 35/c
☎ 075 812821 🖷 075 812502
** **Da Rina** - Piaggia S. Pietro, 20
☎ 075 812817 🖷 075 816824
** **Del Viaggiatore** - Via S. Antonio, 14
☎ 075 816297 🖷 075 813051
** **Excelsior** - Via Tiberio d'Assisi, 2/A
☎ 075 812328 🖷 075 813006
** **Garibaldi** - Piazza Garibaldi, 1
☎ 075 812624 🖷 075 816837
** **Green** - S. Giovanni, 110
Loc. Campiglione
☎ 075 813710 🖷 075 812335
** **Ideale per Turisti** - Piazza Matteotti, 1
☎ 075 813570 🖷 075 813020
** **Il Maniero** - Via S. Pietro Campagna, 32
Loc. S. Fortunato Biagiano
☎ 075 816379 🖷 075 815174
** **Il Palazzo** - Via S. Francesco, 8
☎ 075 816841 🖷 075 812370
** **La Fortezza** - Vicolo della Fortezza
☎ 075 812418 🖷 075 812418
** **La Quiete** - Via S. Pietro Campagna, 95
Loc. Campiglione
☎ 075 812775 🖷 075 812775
** **Lieto Soggiorno** - Via A. Fortini
☎ 075 816191
** **Minerva** - Piazzetta R. Bonghi, 7
☎ 075 812416 🖷 075 813770
** **Pallotta** - Via S. Rufino, 6
☎ 075 812307 🖷 075 812307

** **Posta e Panoramic** - Via S. Paolo, 17
☎ 075 816202 🖷 075 812558
** **Properzio** - Via S. Francesco, 38
☎ 075 813188 🖷 075 815201
** **Roma** - Piazza S. Chiara, 13/15
☎ 075 812390 🖷 075 816743
** **San Giacomo** - Via S. Giacomo, 6
☎ 075 816778 🖷 075 816779
** **San Rufino** - Via Porta Perlici, 7
☎ 075 812803 🖷 075 812803
** **Sole** - Corso Mazzini, 35
☎ 075 812373 🖷 075 813706
** **Villa Elda** - Via S. Pietro Campagna, 139
Fraz. S. Pietro Campagna
☎ 075 8041756 🖷 075 8041501
* **Anfiteatro Romano**
Via Anfiteatro Romano
☎ 075 813025 🖷 075 815110
* **Bellavista** - Via S. Pietro Campagna, 140
Loc. S. Pietro Campagna
☎ 075 8041636 🖷 075 8042492
* **Cavallucci** - Via S. Pietro Campagna
Loc. Ponte S. Vetturino
☎ 075 813279
* **Fontemaggio**
Via Eremo delle Carceri, 8
☎ 075 813636 🖷 075 813749
* **Grotta Antica** - Via Macelli Vecchi, 1
☎ 075 813467
* **Il Duomo** - Vicolo S. Lorenzo, 2
☎ 075 812742 🖷 075 812742
* **Italia** - Vicolo della Fortezza
☎ 075 812625 🖷 075 8043749
* **La Rocca** - Via Porta Perlici, 27
☎ 075 812284 🖷 075 812284
* **Lo Scudo** - Via S. Francesco, 3
☎ 075 813196 🖷 075 813196
* **San Giacomo** - Via S. Giacomo, 4
☎ 075 816778 🖷 075 816779

ASSISI-ARMENZANO
**** **Le Silve** - Via Armenzano, 82
☎ 075 8019000 🖷 075 8019005

ASSISI-PETRIGNANO
*** **La Torretta** - Via del Ponte, 1
☎ 075 8038778 🖷 075 8039474
*** **Poppy Inn** - Via Campagna, 51
☎ 075 8038002 🖷 075 8038002

Assisi-Rivotorto
** Villa Verde - Via Sacro Tugurio, 67
☎ 075 8065444 🖷 075 8064312
* Fontanella - Via S. Maria della Spina, 18
☎ 075 8064400 🖷 075 8064296
* Victor - Via S. Maria della Spina, 1
☎ 075 8064526 🖷 075 8065562
Assisi-San Gregorio
*** Castel S. Gregorio - Via S. Gregorio, 16
☎ 075 8038009 🖷 075 8038904
Assisi-Santa Maria degli Angeli
*** Abacus - Via E. Berlinguer
☎ 075 8043940 🖷 075 8043948
*** Antonelli - Via Los Angeles
☎ 075 8043690 🖷 075 8048028
*** Cristallo - Via Los Angeles
☎ 075 8043094 🖷 075 8043538
*** Dal Moro - Via Santarelli
☎ 075 8043666 🖷 075 8041666
*** Frate Sole
Via S. Bernardino da Siena
☎ 075 8043848 🖷 075 8043828
*** Le Grazie - Via Madonna delle Grazie
☎ 075 8043850 🖷 075 8043851
*** Panda - Via A. Diaz
☎ 075 8043680 🖷 075 8043681
*** Porziuncola - Piazza Garibaldi, 10
☎ 075 8043677 🖷 075 8042890
*** Terra Natia - Via E. Berlinguer, 5
☎ 075 8044193 🖷 075 8044193
** Cenacolo Francescano
Viale Patrono d'Italia, 70
☎ 075 8041083 🖷 075 8040552
** Da Giovanna - Via E. Berlinguer, 14
☎ 075 8043422 🖷 075 8043014
** Domus Pacis - Piazza Porziuncola
☎ 075 8043530 🖷 075 8040455
** Los Angeles - Via Los Angeles
☎ 075 8041339 🖷 075 8041225
** Moderno - Via G. Carducci, 33
☎ 075 8040410 🖷 075 8040647
** Santa Maria - Via Lorenzetti, 2
☎ 075 8041030 🖷 075 8041622
* Dal Moro - Via Becchetti, 11
☎ 075 8041666 🖷 075 8041666
* Donnini - Via Los Angeles, 47
☎ 075 8040260 🖷 075 8040260

* Marconi - Piazza Dante Alighieri, 3
☎ 075 8041156
* Montecavallo - Viale Patrono d'Italia, 46
☎ 075 8040867
* Oasi - Piazza Donegani
☎ 075 8043730 🖷 075 8043730
* Patrono d'Italia - Viale Patrono d'Italia, 48
☎ 075 8040221 🖷 075 8040867
* Porziuncola - Via Micarelli
☎ 075 8043677 🖷 075 8042890
* Vignola - Via S. Bernardino da Siena, 23
☎ 075 8040652 🖷 075 8040652
* Villa Cherubino - Via Patrono d'Italia, 39
☎ 075 8040805 🖷 075 8040226
Bastia umbra
*** Turim - Via Campiglione, 3
☎ 075 8001601
** Campiglione - Via Campiglione, 11
☎ 075 8010767

FARM HOLIDAY CENTERS

Brigolante - Via Costa di Trex, 31
☎ 075 802250 🖷 075 802250
Carfagna Sergio
Via S. Pietro Campagna, 114
☎ 075 813742
Casa del Vento - Az. agr. Frappini
Loc. Porziano, 84
☎ 075 802150 🖷 075 802150
Casa Faustina - Fraz. Mora, 28
☎ 075 8039377 🖷 075 8039377
Casale 3M - Fraz. S. Presto
☎ 075 802178 🖷 075 802178
Casa Nuova - Loc. Pian della Pieve
☎ 075 802143 🖷 075 802143
Casa Rosa - Fraz. S. Maria di Lignano
☎ 075 802322 🖷 075 802322
Col Cacione - Loc. Col Cacione
Fraz. Costa di Trex - ☎ 075 8019010
Corte dei Papi - Via della Fattoria, 48
Passaggio di Bettona - ☎ 075 9889060
Il Castello - Loc. Costa di Trex, 25
☎ 075 813683 🖷 075 813683
Il Girasole - Loc. S. Pietro Campagna, 199
☎ 075 813449 🖷 075 813449
Il Grottino - Via S. Pietro Campagna, 112
☎ 075 816113 🖷 075 816113

Il Mandorlo - Via S. Pietro Campagna, 169
☎ 075 813555 🖷 075 813555
Il Sentiero - Via delle Acacie, 3
☎ 075 8065573 🖷 075 8065573
La Cantina - Via S. Pietro Campagna, 112в
☎ 075 813386 🖷 075 813386
La Castellana - Fraz. Costa di Trex, 50
☎ 075 8019046 🖷 075 8019046
La Palombara - Loc. Costa di Trex
☎ 075 802410 🖷 075 802410
La Panoramica - Via S. Pietro Campagna
Loc. Ponte San Vetturino - ☎ 075 813482
La Piaggia - Ponte San Vetturino, 60
Loc. S. Pietro Campagna
☎ 075 816231 🖷 075 816231
La Pieve - Via Pieve S. Nicolò, 17
☎ 075 8199018 🖷 075 8199018
La Rocca - Fraz. Rocca Sant'Angelo
☎ 075 8039082 🖷 075 8039289
La Selva - Loc. Armenzano
☎ 075 8019057 🖷 075 8019005
Le Antiche Macine - Via S.P. Campagna, 112
☎ 075 812263 🖷 075 812263
Le Cocce - Pian della Pieve, 62
☎ 075 802152 🖷 075 802152
Le Colombe - Loc. Rocca Sant'Angelo, 42
☎ 075 8042421 🖷 075 8042421
Le Querce di Assisi - Pian della Pieve
☎ 075 802332 🖷 075 802500
Longetti - Via S. Pietro Campagna, 35
☎ 075 816175 🖷 075 9869562
Lo Sperone - Loc. Reale, 129
Fraz. Tordandrea
☎ 075 8043257 🖷 075 8043257
Malvarina - Via Malvarina, 32
Loc. Malvarina - ☎ 075 8064280
Miranda - Loc. S. Presto, 94
☎ 075 802130 🖷 075 802130
Nizzi Luigi - Loc. Ponte Grande, 65
☎ 075 813378 🖷 075 813378
Patacca Andrea - San Presto, 113
☎ 075 802222 🖷 075 802222
Podere la Fornace - Via Ombrosa, 3
Loc. Tordibetto
☎ 075 8019537 🖷 075 8019630
San Martino - Via S. Pietro Campagna, 80
☎ 075 813563 🖷 075 813563

Santa Maria della Spina
Loc. Madonna della Spina, 78
☎ 075 9869755 🖷 075 987140
Sasso Rosso - Loc. Capodacqua, 106
☎ 075 8065454 🖷 075 8064861
Siena - Strada della Pescara, 64
Via S. Pietro Campagna
☎ 075 813382 🖷 075 813382
Silvia Letizia - Loc. Costa di Trex
☎ 075 8019008 🖷 075 8019008
Tortoioli Ulderico - Via Casa Madonna, 11
☎ 075 8038806 🖷 075 8038806
Villa Gabbiano - Via Gabbiano, 15
☎ 075 8065278 🖷 075 8065278

CAMP SITES

Fontemaggio - Loc. Fontemaggio
☎ 075 813636 🖷 075 813749
Internazionale Assisi
S. Giovanni in Campiglione, 110
☎ 075 813710 🖷 075 812335

RESTAURANTS-PIZZERIAS

ASSISI
Anfiteatro Romano
Via Teatro Romano, 4 - ☎ 075 815110
Buca di San Francesco - Via Brizi, 1
☎ 075 812204
Camino Vecchio - Via S. Giacomo, 7
☎ 075 812936
Camping - Loc. S. G. Campiglione, 110
☎ 075 813305
Casadei - Via Romana, 43
Capodacqua - ☎ 075 8064133
Centrale Umbra 75 - Via Gorghi, 80
☎ 075 8065455
Da Andrea - Via S. Rufino, 26
☎ 075 815325
Da Boccione - S. Gregorio
☎ 075 8038675-8038438
Da Cecco - Piazza S. Pietro, 8
☎ 075 812437
Da Erminio - Via Montecavallo, 19
☎ 075 812506
Dal Carro - Vocabolo dei Nepis, 2
☎ 075 815249
Dal Moro - Via Ponte Grande - ☎ 075 812969

Degli Orti - Via Salita degli Orti
☎ 075 812549
Dei Consoli - Via Fortezza, 1
☎ 075 812516
Dell'Arco da Bino - Via S. Gregorio, 8
☎ 075 812383-815340
Di Cambio - P.zza Figli di Cambio Palazzo, 6
☎ 075 8030046
Di Sguilla - Viale Marconi, 1
☎ 075 812185-812639
È Pizza - Via Portica, 26 - ☎ 075 813623
Fontemaggio - Via Eremo delle Carceri
☎ 075 812317-813636
Gastronomia - Via Fontebella, 48
☎ 075 812988
Giardino Paradiso
Via Madonna dell'Olivo, 10
☎ 075 812843
Girarrosto La Fortezza
Vocabolo Fortezza, 2 - ☎ 075 812993
Il Caminetto - Via Portica, 29
☎ 075 815126
Il Duomo - Via Porta Perlici, 11
☎ 075 816326
Il Frantoio - Vicolo Illuminati, 10
☎ 075 812883
Il Girasole - Via C. Capodacqua, 67
☎ 075 8043281
Il Menestrello - Via S. Gregorio, 1
☎ 075 812334-816499
I Monaci - Via Scalette Piazzetta Verdi
☎ 075 812512
La Basilica
Via Protomartiri Francescani, 11
☎ 075 8044491
La Lanterna - Via S. Rufino, 41
☎ 075 813142-813217
La Locanda - Via Giotto, 4 - ☎ 075 812121
La Piazzetta
Via S. Gabriele dell'Addolorata, 15
☎ 075 815352
La Rocchicciola - Loc. Rocca S. Angelo
☎ 075 8038161
Manzi Vincenzo - Via S. Rufino, 1
☎ 075 812351
Medio Evo - Via Arco dei Priori, 4/в
☎ 075 813068

Metastasio - Via Metastasio, 9
☎ 075 816525
Millematti - Via Millematti, 16
Viole - ☎ 075 8064175
Mill Garden - Vicolo Illuminati
☎ 075 813225
Otello - Vicolo Sant'Antonio, 1
☎ 075 815125-812415
Pambianco - Viale Michelangelo, 12
Palazzo - ☎ 075 8037102
Pozzo Romano - Via S. Agnese, 10
☎ 075 813057
San Francesco - Via S. Francesco, 52
☎ 075 812329
Siroges - Via del Torrione, 7
☎ 075 816873
Spadini - Via S. Agnese, 6 - ☎ 075 813005

ASSISI-PETRIGNANO
Il Castello di Petrignano
Via del Castello, 2 - ☎ 075 8038565
Locanda del Papavero
Via Indipendenza, 75 - ☎ 075 8038002
Non Solo Pizza - Via Masi, 7
☎ 075 8038296
Trancanelli Aldo - Via Matteotti
☎ 075 8038044

ASSISI-RIVOTORTO
Non Solo Pizza - Via Sacro Tugurio
☎ 075 8064058
Pocoloco - ☎ 075 8064060
Tre Esse Servizio - Via Ghorghi, 3
☎ 075 8064204-8064367-8065132

ASSISI-SANTA MARIA DEGLI ANGELI
Brilli Bistrot Gastronomico
Via Los Angeles - ☎ 075 8043433
Ciccio La Gastronomia - Via A. Diaz
☎ 075 8042956
Feliziani Alberto - Via G. Becchetti
☎ 075 8040291
Il Cantico - Via Patrono d'Italia, 29
☎ 075 8044234
Il Corallo - Via Los Angeles
☎ 075 8040531
Riso Pasquale - Via Los Angeles, 48
☎ 075 8041305
Santucci - Via Patrono d'Italia
☎ 075 8042835

INDEX

Copyright 2001 by Bonechi Edizioni 'Il Turismo' S.r.l.
Via dei Rustici, 5 - 50122 FLORENCE • Tel. +39-055 239.82.24 • Fax +39-055 21.63.66
E-mail: barbara@bonechi.com • bbonechi@dada.it • http://www.bonechi.com
All rights reserved
Printed in Italy

Publishing manager: Barbara Bonechi
Editing of texts and iconographic research: Lorena Lazzari
Graphics and layout: Paola Rufino
English translation: Studio Comunicare
Maps: Bernardo Mannucci for Editing Studio, Pisa
Photo credits: Archives of the Publishing House taken by:
Nicola Grifoni (Florence), Giorgio Deganello (Padua), Marco Rabatti (Florence),
Ferruccio Canali, Giuseppe Carfagna (Rome), Giuliano Valdes (Pisa)
Photographic Archive Sacro Convento of Assisi by Father Gerhard Ruf
Photolithography: Bluprint, Florence
Printing: BO.BA.DO.MA., Florence

ISBN 88-7204-469-3